Literature First
Level B

MODERN CURRICULUM PRESS

Literature First/ *Phonics with a purpose*

Editors: **Linda Lott**
Leslie A. Baranowski
Ann Marie Murray

Contributing Editors: **Catherine E. Crum**
Bonita M. Ferraro
Laraine Walkup Graff
Marian A. Hilliard
Biji Surber Malaker
Margaret Sonnhalter
Irene T. Winslow

Consultant: **Andrea Winters**

Art Director: **John K. Crum**

Cover Art: **Dan Andreason**

Illustrators: Val Mayerik, 5, 9; Holly Kowitt, 11, 19; Clovis Martin, 21, 29; Diana Bridgeman, 31, 39; Zach Safos, 41; Publisher's Graphics, 51, 123, 135; Cheryl Kirk Noll, 53, 61; Creative Studios, 1, 77, 87, 111, 119, 165, 177; Dan Andreasen, 89; Woody Henry, 101; The Art & Design Co., 137, 147, 149, 181, 197; Debbie Palen, 201, 209; Erika Kors, 211, 221.

Acknowledgements: ☐ Excerpt from INDIAN PICTURE WRITING, written and illustrated by Robert Hofsinde (Gray-Wolf). Copyright © 1959 by Robert Hofsinde. By permission of Morrow Junior Books (A Division of William Morrow and Company, Inc.) ☐ ODD JOBS based on a story by Tony Johnston. Copyright © 1977. Reprinted with permission of Writers House. ☐ "Tommy" in *Bronzeville Boys and Girls* by Gwendolyn Brooks. Copyright © 1956 by Gwendolyn Brooks Blakely. Reprinted by permission of Gwendolyn Brooks Blakely. ☐ ANIMAL FACT ANIMAL FABLE by Seymour Simon. Reprinted from: ANIMAL FACT ANIMAL FABLE. Text copyright © 1979 by Seymour Simon. Used by permission of Crown Publishers, Inc. ☐ TY'S ONE-MAN BAND by Mildred Pitts Walter. Reprinted with permission of Four Winds Press, an imprint of Macmillan Publishing Company. Copyright © 1980 by Mildred Pitts Walter. ☐ "A Hikoka in a Hikoki" from IF I HAD A PAKA by Charlotte Pomerantz, text and illustration. Copyright © 1982 by Charlotte Pomerantz. By permission of Greenwillow Books (A Division of William Morrow and Company, Inc.) ☐ THE VERY HUNGRY CATERPILLAR by Eric Carle. Copyright © 1969 by Eric Carle. Reprinted by permission of Philomel Books. ☐ "Laughing Time" by William Jay Smith. Copyright © 1974 by William Jay Smith. Reprinted by permission of DELACORTE PRESS, a division of BANTAM, DOUBLEDAY, DELL PUBLISHING GROUP, INC. ☐ "Johnny Appleseed" by Rosemary and Stephen Vincent Benét from A BOOK OF AMERICANS by Rosemary & Stephen Vincent Benét. Copyright © 1933 by Rosemary & Stephen Vincent Benét. Copyright renewed © 1961 by Rosemary Carr Benét. Reprinted by permission of Brandt & Brandt Literary Agents, Inc. ☐ THE NICEST GIFT by Leo Politi. Reprinted by permission of Charles Scribner's Sons, an imprint of Macmillan Publishing Company from THE NICEST GIFT by Leo Politi. Copyright © 1973 by Leo Politi. ☐ "January" by John Updike from PIPING DOWN THE VALLEYS WILD by Nancy Larrick. Copyright © 1985 by Nancy Larrick. Reprinted by permission of DELACORTE PRESS, a division of BANTAM, DOUBLEDAY, DELL PUBLISHING GROUP, INC. ☐ THERE'S AN ALLIGATOR UNDER MY BED by Mercer Mayer. Copyright © 1987 by Mercer Mayer. Reprinted by permission of the publisher, Dial Books for Young Readers. ☐ FIREFLIES by Julie Brinckloe. Reprinted with permission of Macmillan Publishing Company from FIREFLIES by Julie Brinckloe. Copyright © 1985 by Julie Brinckloe. ☐ "To Meet Mr. Lincoln" from JAMBOREE: Rhymes for All Times by Eve Merriam. Copyright © 1962, 1964, 1966, 1973, 1984 by Eve Merriam. All rights reserved. Reprinted by permission of Marian Reiner for the author. ☐ Abridgement of GOOD-BYE, ARNOLD! by P.K. Roche. Copyright © 1979 by P.K. Roche. Reprinted by permission of the publisher, Dial Books for Young Readers. ☐ FROSTED GLASS by Denys Cazet. Copyright © 1987 by Denys Cazet. Reprinted with permission of Bradbury Press, an imprint of Macmillan Publishing Company. ☐ ALEXANDER AND THE TERRIBLE, HORRIBLE, NO GOOD, VERY BAD DAY by Judith Viorst. Text copyright © 1972 by Judith Viorst. Reprinted with permission of Atheneum Publishers, an imprint of Macmillan Publishing Company. ☐ "Oh Dear!" by Biji Surber Malaker. Copyright © 1988. Reprinted by permission of Biji Surber Malaker. Every effort has been made to trace ownership of all copyrighted material in this book and obtain permission for its use.

MODERN CURRICULUM PRESS, INC.
A Division of Simon & Schuster
13900 Prospect Road, Cleveland, Ohio 44136

ISBN 0-8136-0320-X

9 10 11   93 94 95 96

Table of Contents

Indian Picture Writing

Picture writing is a way of expressing thoughts and recording events by marks or drawings. The American Indians used picture writing to tell their legends and dreams, personal triumphs in the hunt and on the battlefield, and family and tribal history.

It is easy to develop skill in the art of picture writing, and boys and girls today can have fun using it for secret messages.

— Robert Hofsinde (Gray-Wolf)

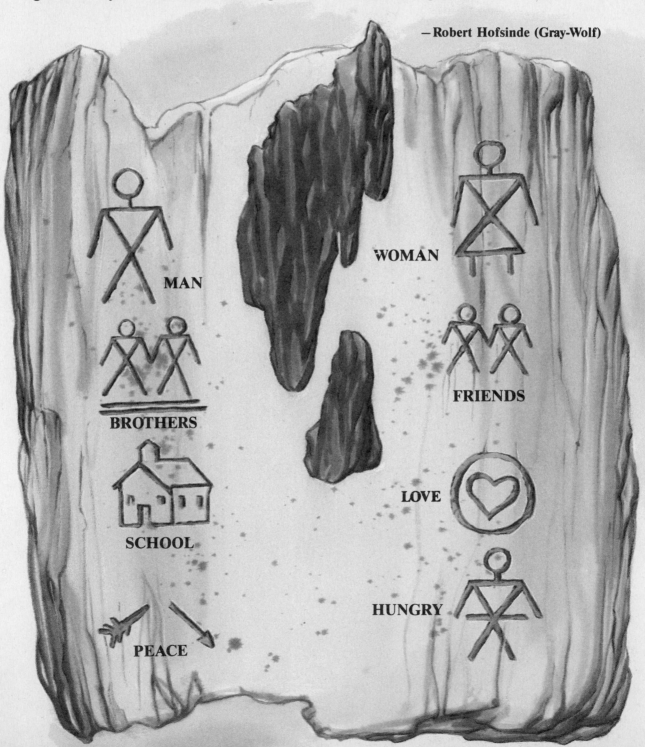

Picture writing can be fun! When you write with pictures you do not even need an alphabet. Make up your own symbols for the words below.

BROTHERS   SCHOOL   HUNGRY

SISTERS   HOUSE   FULL

LOOK   SLEEP   STOP

At the Library 📖

Signs and codes are what these books are all about.
Koko's Kitten by Francine Patterson
Secret Codes by Helen Jill Fletcher

Today we write with the alphabet instead of pictures.
Use the clues to find the word each picture stands for.
Write it on the line.

A B C D E F G H I J K L M N O P Q R S T U V W X Y Z

1.

I am the opposite of <u>me</u>.
My first letter comes just before <u>z</u>.

I am _____.

2.

My first letter comes between <u>g</u> and <u>i</u>.
You may live in me.

I am a _____.

3.

My first letter comes just before <u>m</u>.
You may see me in a rainstorm.

I am _____.

4.

My first letter comes just after <u>a</u>.
I help keep you warm at night.

I am a _____.

5.

My first letter comes between <u>n</u> and <u>p</u>.
I am a month when leaves fall.

I am _____.

Family Activity

Make up your own picture symbol. Write a riddle about it.
Be sure to use an alphabet clue! See if your family can
solve it.

_____

_____

_____

Play tic-tac-toe. Say each letter. Draw a straight line through three letters in each game that are in alphabetical order. You can go across, down, or corner to corner.

a	b	d
c	f	a
d	e	f

h	j	k
i	i	l
g	m	j

r	s	n
n	o	p
q	r	t

u	y	w
v	z	x
x	w	y

Challenge

Write these words in alphabetical order: mail, tent, lamp, cart.

_____

_____

Write a message to a friend using picture symbols. Then on another sheet of paper decode your message using words.

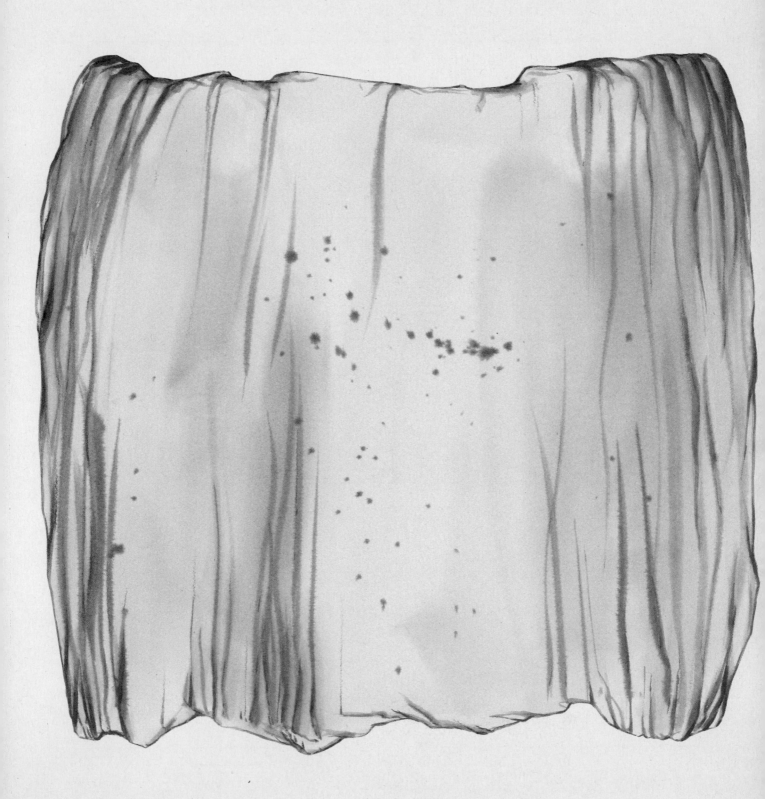

Read each group of words. Then fill in the circle under the words that are in alphabetical order.

1. ball, desk, cat   ant, bath, cap   cold, bed, dish
    ○   ○   ○

2. fish, can, dig   dog, ear, fan   bag, goat, fill
    ○   ○   ○

3. frog, girl, end   eat, door, gift   egg, fall, game
    ○   ○   ○

4. jump, hill, ice   house, in, jet   kite, hop, igloo
    ○   ○   ○

5. kit, lion, mask   new, meet, look   list, kick, moon
    ○   ○   ○

6. note, pal, old   need, open, pan   men, ocean, neat
    ○   ○   ○

7. pet, quiet, race   read, queen, send   quilt, sun, ride
    ○   ○   ○

8. two, soap, ugly   sad, time, rain   sand, ten, under
    ○   ○   ○

9. tap, until, vest   tree, vote, sail   went, vent, yarn
    ○   ○   ○

10. yes, zebra, wish   wait, x-ray, you   yoyo, zoo, week
    ○   ○   ○

Odd Jobs

"My dog, Bouncer, needs a bath," said Dolly Finch. "Can you do the job?"

"Sure," said Odd Jobs. Then Bouncer came out. Odd Jobs went home and went to work. He filled the sink and called Bouncer. Bouncer came and drank all the water.

He filled a tub and floated a dog biscuit in the middle. PLOP! Bouncer jumped in and sat on the dog biscuit. So Odd Jobs washed him fast. Bouncer bounced out of the tub and stood very still.

"All right," said Odd Jobs. "Now stay clean."

So Bouncer jumped over him, skated across the garage, galloped into the garden, and dug up the flowers.

Odd Jobs sneaked up behind him with the tub. "This time you'll stay clean if I have to carry you home."

When the bath was over, Odd Jobs wrapped Bouncer in a beach towel and carried him. Then Bouncer started chewing on the towel. He stopped that and started chewing on Odd Jobs. So he stopped carrying him — ooph. And, sure enough, Bouncer was dirty again.

"Hi, Dolly," puffed Odd Jobs.

Dolly Finch looked at Bouncer and said, "He's the dirtiest dog I ever saw."

"Well," said Odd Jobs. "Under all that dirt is the cleanest dog you ever saw."

— Tony Johnston

Odd Jobs found a job washing Dolly's dog. What are some jobs you can do? Write their names on the lines. Then draw a picture of yourself doing one of the jobs.

_____

_____

_____

_____

_____

_____

_____

At the Library 📖

Would you like to read more about people and their jobs? Try these books.

Juan Patricio by Barbara K. Todd

Amelia Bedelia by Peggy Parish

Read the sentences from the story. Some of the words are missing. Fill in the missing words so the sentences make sense.

1. _____ _____ went home and went

   to _____.

2. Bouncer bounced out of the tub and stood _____ still.

3. "All right," said Odd Jobs. "_____ stay _____."

4. Bouncer _____ into the garden and _____ up the flowers.

5. Odd Jobs _____ up behind him with the _____.

6. "This time _____ stay clean if I have to carry

   _____ home."

7. "He's the dirtiest dog I _____ saw."

8. _____ all that dirt is the _____ dog you ever saw.

Family Activity

Dolly's dog Bouncer needs baths, but he needs lots of other things, too. Ask your family to help you make a list of things pets need. Underline the letters **g**, **k**, **n**, **y**, **v**, **x**, **z**, **o**, and **u** in your list. Look for those letters in other words.

g, k, n, y, v, x, z	Say the name of the picture. Listen for the sounds of **g**, **k**, **n**, **y**, **v**, **x**, and **z**. Use a crayon to trace the letter that stands for each sound.

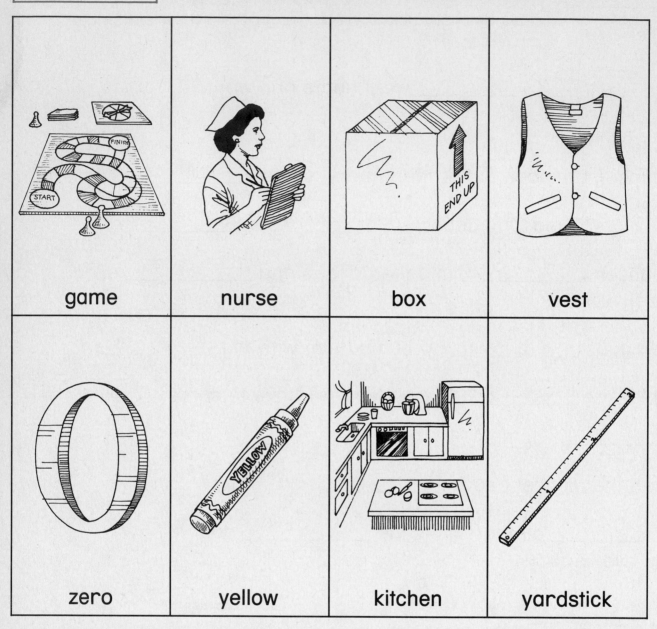

game	nurse	box	vest
zero	yellow	kitchen	yardstick

Think of more words that have the sound of **g**, **k**, **n**, **y**, **v**, **x**, or **z**. Write them on the lines.

1. _____   5. _____

2. _____   6. _____

3. _____   7. _____

4. _____   8. _____

When a single vowel comes at the beginning of a word or between two consonants, it usually has a short sound. The word jobs has the sound of short **o**. The word pup has the sound of short **u**.

Read the story below. Circle the short **o** words. Underline the short **u** words.

It was a hot summer day. A thirsty Fox trotted in the sun. He spotted a bunch of juicy grapes.

"Those grapes would taste just as good as water," he thought.

But the grape vine hung on a high branch. Fox jumped into the air, but he could not reach them. He tried and tried. Finally he gave up.

"I didn't want those rotten grapes anyway," grumbled the Fox. "I'll bet they are sour."

Moral: Do not hate what you cannot have.

Challenge

Write a sentence that tells the main idea of the fable. Try to use some short **o** and short **u** words.

_____

_____

_____

Unscramble the words under each sentence. Write them in the correct order on the line. Read your sentences. Do they make sense?

1. Odd Jobs was not too _____.

   work   young   to

2. He thought bathing Bouncer would be

   a _____.

   job   good   very

3. Sometimes he washes his _____.

   mother's   car   new

4. He takes younger children to _____.

   the   visit   zoo

5. Aunt Lucy lets Odd Jobs take her dog _____.

   a   walk   for

6. After school, he is glad _____.

   errands   to   run

7. He is always willing to mop _____.

   or   scrub   to

8. Would you like Odd Jobs to _____?

   for   you   work

Challenge

Make up your own scrambled sentence. Let a friend unscramble the words.

Cut out the flash cards. Practice reading the words with a partner.

Time to Write

Write sentences about jobs you would like. Use words from the cards.

gobble

box

kids

clock

never

zero

yell

lunch

voice

scrub

mix	giggle
mop	key
puzzle	number
plus	yardstick
stuck	vowels

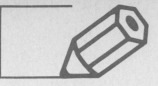

Write a story about a job that looks easy but turns out to be hard. Who is the main character? What is the job? Why did you think it would be an easy job? What happens to make it hard?

_____

_____

_____

_____

_____

_____

_____

_____

_____

_____

_____

_____

_____

_____

_____

Say the name of each picture. Fill in the circle under the word that has the same vowel sound.

1.

click	fun	spot	back
○	○	○	○

2.

sunny	branch	doctor	swing
○	○	○	○

3.

yes	sub	bench	door
○	○	○	○

4.

knock	win	desk	swamp
○	○	○	○

Read each sentence that has been started for you. Then fill in the circle under the word that completes the sentence.

5. After lunch, you may play kickball in the _____.

yawn	yard	zigzag	vest
○	○	○	○

6. Then the class will have a spelling _____.

vine	grip	zoo	quiz
○	○	○	○

7. I hope you have a very _____ day.

vine	good	wax	get
○	○	○	○

8. Many people _____ at your school.

will	kitten	six	work
○	○	○	○

TOMMY

I put a seed into the ground
And said, "I'll watch it grow."
I watered it and cared for it
As well as I could know.

One day I walked in my backyard,
And oh, what did I see!
My seed had popped itself right out,
Without consulting me.

—Gwendolyn Brooks

Have you ever planted seeds and watched them grow? On the lines below, list all the kinds of seeds you can think of. Draw a picture of a plant you would like to grow.

Would you like to know more about how things grow?
Try these books.
Corn Is Maize: The Gift of the Indians by Aliki

Pumpkin, Pumpkin by Jeanne Titherington

Read the poem. Some of the words are missing. Fill in the missing words so the poem makes sense.

1. I put a _____ into the ground

2. And _____, "I'll watch it grow."

3. I watered it and _____ for it

4. As _____ as I could know.

5. One day I walked in my _____,

6. And oh, what _____ I see!

7. My seed had _____ itself right out,

8. Without consulting me.

Family Activity

Ask your family to help you think of kinds of plants you can grow from a seed. Make a list of plants whose names start with **s, w, d, p, c, r,** or **b**.

Read each word. Change the first letter to make rhyming words. Use **s**, **w**, **d**, **p**, **c**, **r**, or **b**.

1. Bill _____ _____ _____

2. rest _____ _____ _____

3. pin _____ _____ _____

4. sent _____ _____ _____

5. wit _____ _____ _____

6. dig _____ _____ _____

7. sink _____ _____ _____

8. dell _____ _____ _____

Challenge

Choose two rhyming words from your list. Use them to write a short poem.

_____

_____

_____

_____

When a single vowel comes at the beginning of a word or between two consonants, it usually has a short sound. The word *wet* has the sound of short **e**. *Win* has the sound of short **i**.

Read the fable below. Circle the short **e** words. Underline the short **i** words.

The day was hot and sunny. A hard-working ant carried food to its nest. The ant passed a grasshopper playing in the sun.

"Stop and rest," said the grasshopper.

"The cold, wet winter is on the way. You'd better get busy and store up some food," replied the ant.

The grasshopper winked and danced a jig. "Why worry?" it laughed. "I have all I need. It's too nice to work."

Kicking up its heels, the grasshopper sped away.

But the grim, chilly winter did come. The ant was warm. It had plenty of food. The hungry grasshopper shivered in the snow and hoped the ant would share its food.

Choose some of the short **e** and short **i** words from the story. Use them to tell what lesson the fable teaches.

_____

_____

_____

_____

_____

_____

_____

_____

Unscramble the words under each sentence. Write them in the correct order on the lines.

1. Do you know how to _____?

   garden   a   grow

2. Get the soil ready and _____.

   the   pull   weeds

3. You can plant fruit, vegetables, _____.

   or • plants   flowering

4. Maybe you would like to grow _____.

   pumpkin   big   a

5. After planting your garden, it's time _____.

   a   for   rest

6. Gardeners are always on the_____.

   bugs   for   lookout

7. Every garden _____.

   good   needs   care

8. What would you _____?

   like   grow   to

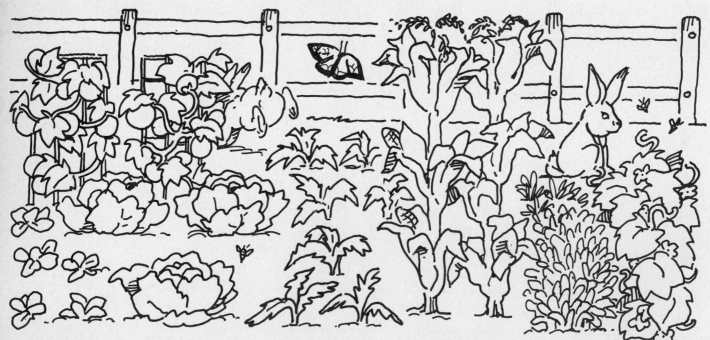

Challenge

Make up your own scrambled sentence. Let a friend try to unscramble it.

Cut out the flash cards. Illustrate five of the words.
Choose a partner to put the correct flash card on each
picture.

Time to Write ✏

Make up sentences about caring for plants. Leave out one
flash card word. Let a friend guess the missing word.

sun

water

dirt

plant

cared

rake

beans

stem

did

well

watch   seeds

pot   day

roots   can

smell   basket

help   pick

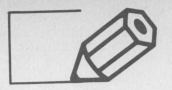

What do you think it would be like to be a tiny seed waiting to grow? Pretend you are a little seed that has just been planted. What do you need? What are you thinking as you wait in the ground? What happens when you finally "pop out"?

_____

_____

_____

_____

_____

_____

_____

_____

_____

_____

_____

Say the name of each picture. Fill in the circle under the word that has the same vowel sound.

1.				
	pin ○	plant ○	what ○	run ○

2.				
	east ○	past ○	nine ○	best ○

3.				
	arctic ○	grow ○	seed ○	pillow ○

4.				
	pet ○	rinse ○	beads ○	cane ○

Read each sentence that has been started for you. Then fill in the circle under the word that completes the sentence.

5. Do you like to play outside in the _____?

wish	grass	play	big
○	○	○	○

6. A seed is like a plant's _____.

picnic	baby	dirt	window
○	○	○	○

7. When you plant a seed, give it _____.

blankets	milk	water	wind
○	○	○	○

8. A seed grows up to be a _____.

plant	puppy	bear	dinosaur
○	○	○	○

Animal Fact, Animal Fable

Even if you watch animals closely, it is sometimes easy to mistake what is happening. For example, a bat flutters around in an odd way in the night sky. Some people may think that bats are blind and can't see where they are going.

If bats are really blind, that belief is true; it is a fact. But suppose the bat flies in that odd way for another reason, and is not really blind. Then the belief is a fable; it is not true.

GOATS WILL EAT ALMOST ANYTHING

FACT Goats will eat almost anything they can find. They even seem to eat tin cans. But they are not really eating the metal can; they are chewing the label to get at the glue underneath.

Though goats eat string and paper, they would rather eat fruit, vegetables, grass, and leaves of plants. They are not quite the "garbage cans" some people think they are.

RACCOONS WASH THEIR FOOD

FABLE Raccoons sometimes dip their food into water before they eat, but they are not washing it. A raccoon's throat is not very large. It has trouble swallowing large pieces of food. Dipping food in water makes it softer and easier to swallow. When a raccoon finds a mushy piece of fruit, he doesn't wash it no matter how dirty it is. He just gulps it down right away.

—Seymour Simon

A fact is a statement that is true. Use facts you know about your favorite animals to complete the map below.

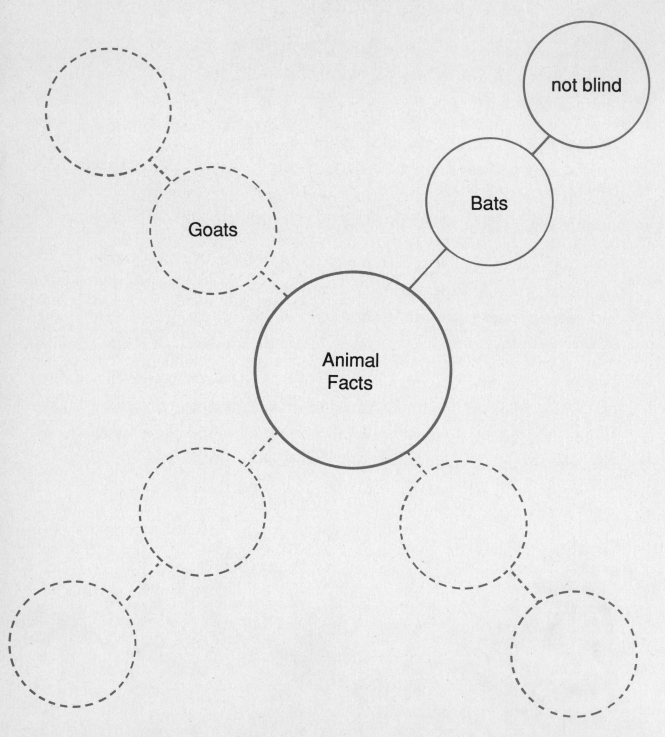

At the Library 📖

Learn more interesting animal facts from these books.
<u>The Butterfly Cycle</u> by John Cooke

<u>Watching Them Grow: Inside a Zoo Nursery</u> by Joan Hewett

Read the sentences from the story. Some of the words are missing. Fill in the missing words so the sentences make sense.

1. Goats will eat _____ anything they can _____.

2. They even seem to eat _____ cans.

3. They are not _____ the "garbage _____" some people think they are.

4. Raccoons sometimes dip their _____ into water before they eat, but they are not washing it.

5. A _____ throat is not very large.

6. It has trouble swallowing _____ pieces of food.

7. When a raccoon finds a _____ piece of fruit, he doesn't wash it no matter _____ dirty it is.

8. He _____ gulps it down right away.

Family Activity

Ask your family to help you make a list of words that have the sound of **f**, **h**, **j**, **l**, **m**, **q**, **t**, or **a**. Use two of the words to make up a sentence about animals.

f, h, j, l,
m, q, t, a

Play double tic-tac-toe. Say the name of each picture. Use a red crayon to draw a straight line through three pictures whose names have the first sound. Use a blue crayon to draw a straight line through three pictures whose names have the second sound. You can go across, down, or corner to corner.

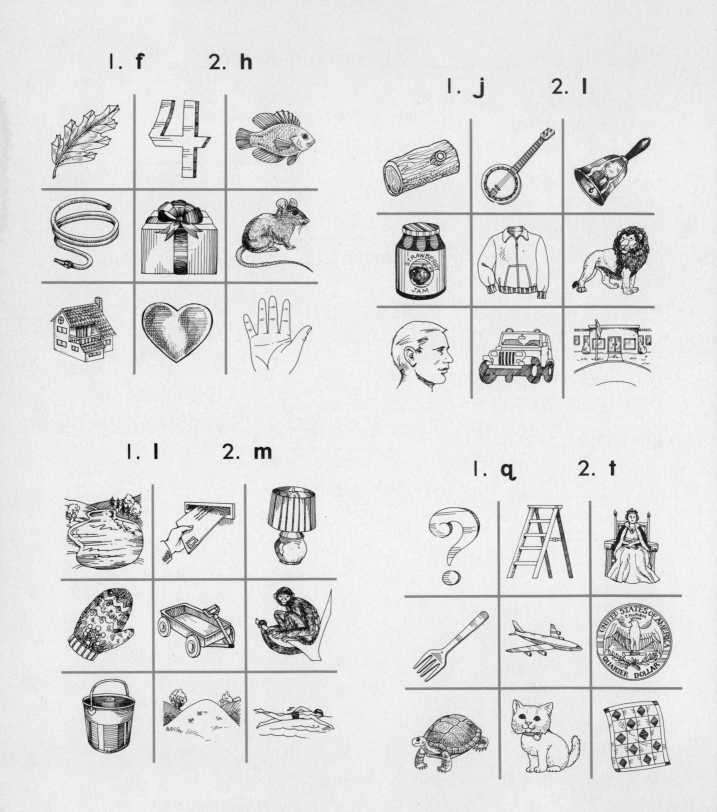

1. **f**   2. **h**

1. **j**   2. **l**

1. **l**   2. **m**

1. **q**   2. **t**

Read each riddle. Write the missing word on the line.
Each answer has the sound of short **a**.

1. I am the name for all of these:
   A cat, a dog, a mouse, a horse.

   I am an _____.

2. I always know the way to go.
   Follow me and you won't get lost.

   I am a _____.

3. I wear a shade upon my head.
   You can turn me on and off.

   I am a _____.

4. In the spring I'm nice and green.
   In the winter I'm covered with white.

   I am the _____.

5. I am the color you see when you turn out the light.
   I am the color of the deep, dark night.

   I am _____.

6. When it's cold you do not need me.
   When it's hot you need me a lot.

   I am a _____.

7. When the sun is out I follow you about.
   But in the shade I go away.

   I am your _____.

8. I don't leave letters alone.
   You always put me in the corner.

   I am a _____.

Read each sentence. Circle the word that completes the sentence. Write the word on the line.

1. There are many more _____ fables.

    lamp
    animal
    fact

2. One such fable is that an _____ is a very wise bird.

    owl
    hamster
    bats

3. Some people think a camel's _____ stores water, but it does not.

    hand
    last
    hump

4. If you think porcupines can really shoot their _____, you're wrong.

    quick
    food
    quills

5. The idea that a wolf lives alone is _____ a fable.

    just
    jam
    fast

6. You may have heard that a _____ gets mad when he sees the color red.

    hill
    land
    bull

7. Another fable is that a _____ can walk out of its shell.

    tap
    quack
    turtle

Challenge

Write your own fable about a monkey. Share it with a friend.

_____

_____

Cut out the flash cards. Take turns with a partner saying a sentence for each flash card word.

Time to Write ✏️

Write sentences about animals. Use words on your cards.

home	calf
last	jam
quick	makes
fact	turtle
tracks	grass

fast	has
jump	land
camel	quiet
eating	animal
bats	rabbit

Choose an animal you know about. Write a fact or a fable about it. Let a partner read your story and guess whether it is fact or fable.

_____

_____

_____

_____

_____

_____

_____

_____

_____

Test Lesson 4	Say the word in each row. Look at the letter in the box. Then fill in the circle under the picture whose name has the same sound as the boxed letter.

1. ba[t]s

○ ○ ○ ○

2. [q]uilt

○ ○ ○ ○

3. [h]ill

○ ○ ○ ○

4. fl[a]g

○ ○ ○ ○

5. [j]ump

○ ○ ○ ○

6. ha[m]

○ ○ ○ ○

7. gi[f]t

○ ○ ○ ○

8. [l]and

○ ○ ○ ○

Ty's One-man Band

The grass grew tall enough to hide a boy as big as Ty. He lay quiet, listening. Step-th-hump . . . Then Ty saw a man. The man had only one leg. The other one was nothing but a wooden peg.

"Who are you?" asked Ty.

"My name is Andro. I'm a one-man band. Go home and get a washboard and two wooden spoons, a tin pail and a comb. I'll come into town at sundown and make music for you and your friends."

No one believed there was such a thing as a one-man band. All of Ty's friends laughed. Ty sat on the corner. Then he heard a step-th-hump, step-th-hump, step-th-hump. He was coming.

"Whee-ee-ttt!" Andro whistled. He placed the spoons between his fingers and moved them very fast. Quack-quack-quacket-t-quack. The music drifted through the empty streets, around quiet corners. One by one people began to leave their porches.

Andro set the pail down. With a spoon in his hand, he hit the pail, his wooden leg, and the other spoon. Di-de-le-dum, di-de-le-dum, de-di-la-di-ti-do, de-di-la-de-ti-do, chuck-chick-chu-dum, chuck-chick-chu-dum, chuck-chick-chu-dum.

Boys and girls, mothers and fathers, even the babies clapped their hands. Everybody danced.

—Mildred Pitts Walter

Andro did not use real instruments like drums or horns to make his one-man band. He used things like spoons and a pail to make music. What else could Andro have used? Make a map of things you could use to make your own one-man band.

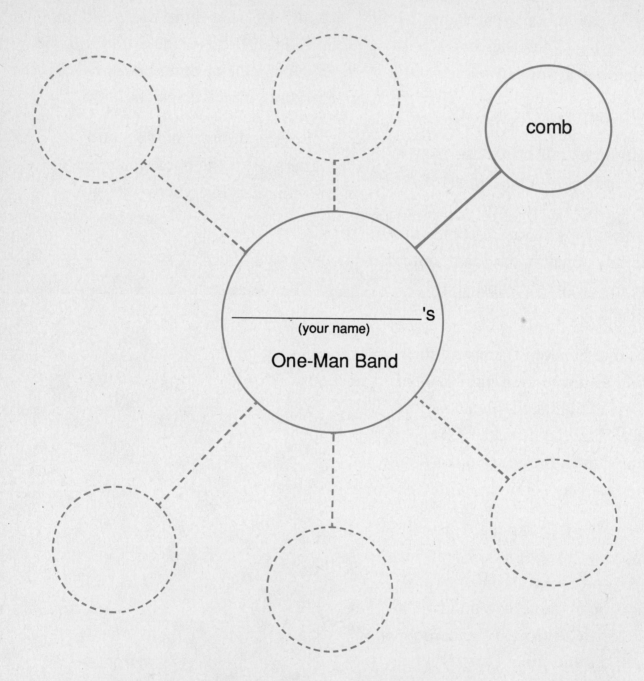

comb

_____'s
(your name)
One-Man Band

At the Library

Read more about things you can do with musical instuments.

<u>The Bremen Town Musicians</u> by Jakob and Wilhelm Grimm

<u>The Riddle of the Drum: A Tale from Tizipan, Mexico</u> by Verna Aardema

Read the sentences from the story. Some of the words are missing. Fill in the missing words so the sentences make sense.

1. "My name is _____. I'm a one man band."

2. "_____ _____ and get a washboard, two wooden spoons, a tin pail and a comb."

3. "I'll make _____ for you and your friends."

4. _____ one believed there was such a thing.

5. "Whee-ee-ttt!" _____ whistled.

6. The _____ drifted through the empty streets.

7. _____ set the pail down.

Family Activity

Share these musical riddles with your family. Tell them the answers are long **o** or long **u** words.

1. What did the skeleton play in the band?   bones

2. Over the holidays, what did the musician eat for dessert?   flutecake

Ask your family to help you write more musical riddles.
Use long **o** and long **u** words.

Read the words in the box. Listen for the sound of long **o**. Write each word in the correct column.

home	show	oak	piano	over	those
road	go	whole	known	throat	own

oa **o-e** **ow** **o**

_____ _____ _____ _____

_____ _____ _____ _____

_____ _____ _____ _____

Challenge

Work with a partner to add your own words to the lists above.

_____ _____ _____ _____

_____ _____ _____ _____

_____ _____ _____ _____

_____ _____ _____ _____

_____ _____ _____ _____

Read the fable to find out how the crow brought music to the forest. Then read the fable again. Circle the long **o** words and underline the long **u** words.

The weather was not usual for July. No rain had fallen in the forest. The birds were too thirsty to chirp out any tunes. The crow set out to find water. He wanted to bring music back to the forest.

The crow flew until he spotted a huge pitcher with a little water at the bottom. But the neck of the pitcher was so narrow he couldn't even get his beak inside. The crow could see the water, but he couldn't drink it. He thought and thought. What could he use to get the water?

Finally he had an idea. He picked up small stones and dropped them one by one into the pitcher. Little by little the water rose. Soon it was near enough to the top.

"Caw, caw, caw!" he sang. "I have found water. I will go and get the other birds. We will have music in the forest again."

Challenge

What lesson does the fable teach?

_____

_____

_____

_____

_____

_____

_____

_____

Read each rhyme. Write the missing long **o** or long **u** word on the line.

1. My glass is shaped just like a tube.

   There's only room for one ice _____.

2. Herbie thinks that he looks cute,

   Marching with his shiny _____.

3. Stay away from burning fuel.

   That is just a safety _____.

4. That very old dinosaur _____
   Looks like it is made of stone.

5. If Mom says "_____!"
   Then, we can't go!

6. On my math test I missed _____,
   So my dad says I'm a hero.

7. Use your _____
   To smell this red rose.

8. I broke the motor on Sam's mower.

   Now, it moves a little _____.

Challenge

Write a rhyme about music. Use a pair of long **o** or long **u**
words like:

        vote - note   tune - June

_____

_____

Cut out the flash cards. Tell a partner the letter or letters that stand for the sound of long **o** or long **u** in each word.

Time to Write ✏

Pick two words. Write a list of words that rhyme with the words you have chosen.

grow

fruit

bone

menu

soak

uniform

open

January

yellow

unit

music	load
use	so
mule	vote
universe	know
United States	float

Where do you think Andro came from? Where did he go when he left Ty's town? Write a story that tells about another day in Andro's life.

Read each clue. Write the long **o** or long **u** word in the correct place in the puzzle.

ACROSS
1. a long, flat piece of wood
4. opposite of high
5. a song
6. an instrument shaped like a pipe

DOWN
2. what you use to measure
3. a horn like a trumpet

Challenge

What long **u** word in the puzzle could you use as a drumstick?

_____

What long **u** words could you play in a band?

_____   _____

Use a long **o** word to complete this sentence.

Joan sang the high notes and Tom sang the _____ notes.

Say the name of each picture. Fill in the circle under the word that has the same vowel sound.

1.

just	music	puddle	funny
○	○	○	○

2.

float	job	town	zoo
○	○	○	○

3.

slot	drop	go	could
○	○	○	○

4.

huge	mud	branch	up
○	○	○	○

5.

puppy	pupil	cut	hunt
○	○	○	○

6.

coat	lock	box	top
○	○	○	○

7.

us	bud	stuck	cute
○	○	○	○

Read each sentence that has been started for you. Then fill in the circle under the word that completes the sentence.

1. The soccer _____ told us the rules of the game.

catch	coach	clock	cot
○	○	○	○

2. Do I need a _____ for math today?

rust	ruler	rude	punch
○	○	○	○

3. We looked for our state on the _____.

globe	robe	rock	coin
○	○	○	○

4. Janet wanted to _____ bean seeds.

brown	stop	come	grow
○	○	○	○

5. Gino played a _____ in the school band.

flute	thumb	suit	bus
○	○	○	○

6. The most snow fell in _____.

August	tube	summer	January
○	○	○	○

7. Please _____ quickly when the fire bell rings.

go	got	golf	good
○	○	○	○

8. Read the _____ before you order dinner.

menu	lunch	number	cube
○	○	○	○

A HIKOKA IN A HIKOKI

Whenever someone asks me what I want to be,
I answer a hikoka in a hikoki:
A pilot in an airplane—brave, alone and free.
Unless, of course, I chanced to meet another kid, and she,
Whenever someone asked her what she would like to be,
Answered a hikoka in a hikoki.
In which case—oh, what fun!—she could fly the plane with me.

—Charlotte Pomerantz

Look up in the sky. Do you see a hikoki? On the lines below write the names of some other things you might see flying in the sky.

HIKOKI

Things that can fly...

_____

_____

_____

_____

_____

At the Library 📖

Read more about flying.
The Berenstain Bears on the Moon by Stan and Jan Berenstain
The Emperor and the Kite by Jane Yolen

Read the poem. Some of the words are missing. Fill in the missing words so the poem makes sense.

1. Whenever someone asks _____ what I want

   to _____,

2. _____ answer a hikoka in a hikoki:

3. A _____ in an airplane—brave, alone,

   and _____ .

4. Unless, of course, I chanced to _____ another

   kid and _____,

5. Whenever someone asked her what she would _____

   to _____,
   Answered a hikoka in a hikoki.

6. In which case—oh, what fun!—_____ could fly the

   plane with _____ .

Family Activity

Make a list of long **i** or long **e** words. Draw a picture of
your favorite word. Share your list with the class.

When a word ends in **e**, the first vowel usually has a long sound and the final **e** is usually silent. *Like* is a long **i** word.

Read each rhyme. Write the missing long **i** word on the line.

1. Kelly will be sure to like

   Riding on her ten-speed _____.

2. Let's go! Run and hide

   Behind the fence on the other _____.

3. We raked and raked for quite a while.

   At last the leaves were in a _____.

4. It looks as if the bees will dive,

   Buzzing into their big _____.

5. "We will have a super life,"

   Said the groom to his new _____.

6. Keep it warm. That is wise.

   Or else the bread won't start to _____.

7. We watched the workmen paint a stripe

   On that huge piece of iron _____.

Challenge

Write a rhyme about something that flies. Use a pair of long **i** words like **kite** and **white**.

_____

_____

Long e

Do you think only pilots go up in the sky? Read the poem to find out what Mother Goose saw in the sky.

Then circle the long **e** words in the poem. Look for two vowels together or a single vowel at the end of a word. *Geese* and *me* are long **e** words.

There was an old woman toss'd up in a basket
Nineteen times as high as the moon;
Where she was going I couldn't but ask it,
For in her hand she carried a broom.

"Old woman, old woman, old woman," quoth I,
"O whither, O whither, O whither, so high?"
"To sweep the cobwebs off the sky!"
"Shall I go with thee?" "Ay, by-and-by."

What was the woman trying to do? Draw a picture to show your answer.

Write the name of the picture on the line to complete each sentence.

1. The airplane landed at _____ o'clock.

2. Mike let go of his pretty _____ balloon.

3. The traffic helicopter flew over the busy _____.

4. We saw sea gulls flying over the sandy _____.

5. The blimp had red and white _____ on its side.

6. The bees swarmed to make honey in their _____.

7. A bald _____ soars high above the mountains.

8. The _____ had a long, colorful tail.

Challenge

Draw a picture. Write a sentence with a missing word. Let
a partner write in the answer.

Cut out the flash cards. Spell each word to a partner.
Then sort the cards into a long **i** pile and a long **e** pile.

Time to Write

Write a story about where you would go if you were able to fly.

kite	she
glides	see
dives	trees
spider	meet
find	leaf

me

like

free

lion

bees

time

eagle

tiny

reach

pilot

Would you like to be a *hikoka* in a *hikoki* when you grow up? Or would you like to be something else? Write a poem or a story that tells what you would like to be and what you would do.

Whenever someone asks me
What I want to be

I answer _____

_____

_____

_____

_____

_____

_____

_____

_____

_____

_____

_____

Read each sentence. Write the missing long **i** or long **e** word on the line.

1. The ◯____ ____ ____ ____ light meant go.

2. So, the ____ ____◯____ ____ started the little plane.

3. Next, she had to ____◯____ ____ some water off the window.

4. Then, she had to ____ ____ ____◯ the map one more time.

5. "Now, ____◯____ are ready to take off," she shouted.

6. "Let's ◯____ ____ ____ high into the clouds!"

Write the circled letters on the lines to name something that flies.

____ ____ ____ ____ ____ ____
 1   2   3   4   5   6

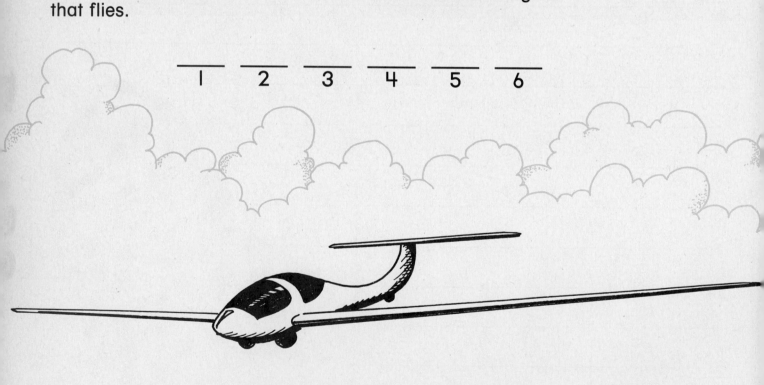

Say the name of each picture. Fill in the circle under the word that has the same vowel sound.

1.

less	he	help	egg
○	○	○	○

2.

write	is	gift	inch
○	○	○	○

3.

bread	end	peach	let
○	○	○	○

4.

we	well	dress	next
○	○	○	○

5.

miss	tiny	which	dig
○	○	○	○

6.

ill	give	strike	lift
○	○	○	○

7.

set	when	left	deep
○	○	○	○

Read each sentence that has been started for you. Then fill in the circle under the word that completes the sentence.

1. Are the apples _____ yet?

     gift   ripe   inch   like
     ○   ○   ○   ○

2. The baby bear's bed was just the right _____.

     quilt   size   with   little
     ○   ○   ○   ○

3. _____ everything on your plate.

     Meal   Spell   Help   Eat
     ○   ○   ○   ○

4. The _____ put on her purple robe.

     pretty   queen   next   read
     ○   ○   ○   ○

5. My desk is 20 inches long and 16 inches _____.

     wide   since   bike   which
     ○   ○   ○   ○

6. Let's _____ through the woods.

     wish   tie   into   hike
     ○   ○   ○   ○

7. Can you _____ a secret?

     keep   red   end   meet
     ○   ○   ○   ○

8. _____ is my little brother.

     Them   He   Elf   Bee
     ○   ○   ○   ○

The Very Hungry Caterpillar

In the light of the moon a little egg lay on a leaf. One Sunday morning the warm sun came up and—pop!—out of the egg came a tiny and very hungry caterpillar.

He started to look for some food. On Monday he ate through one apple. But he was still hungry. On Tuesday he ate through two pears, but he was still hungry.

On Wednesday he ate through three plums, but he was still hungry. On Thursday he ate through four strawberries, but he was still hungry.

On Friday he ate through five oranges, but he was still hungry. On Saturday he ate through one piece of chocolate cake, one ice-cream cone, one pickle, one slice of Swiss cheese, one slice of salami, one lollipop, one piece of cherry pie, one sausage, one cupcake, and one slice of watermelon. That night he had a stomachache!

The next day was Sunday again. The caterpillar ate through one nice green leaf, and after that he felt much better. Now he wasn't hungry any more and he wasn't a little caterpillar anymore. He was a big, fat caterpillar.

He built a small house, called a cocoon, around himself. He stayed inside for more than two weeks. Then he nibbled a hole in the cocoon, pushed his way out and . . . he was a beautiful butterfly!

— Eric Carle

The very hungry caterpillar turned into a butterfly when he grew up. That was a big change! Other living creatures change, too, and so do their names. A child grows up to be an adult. A kitten grows up to be a cat.

Write the names for baby animals on the lines on the left. Write what they grow into on the lines on the right. Work with a partner if you wish.

_____   _____

_____   _____

_____   _____

_____   _____

_____   _____

_____   _____

_____   _____

At the Library 📖

To find out more about animals growing up, read these books.

How Puppies Grow by Millicent E. Selsam

I Can Read About Creepy Crawly Creatures by C. J. Naden

Read the sentences from the story. Some of the words are missing. Fill in the blanks so the sentences make sense.

1. A little egg _____ on a leaf.

2. One Sunday morning the warm sun _____ up.

3. Out of the egg came a _____ and _____ hungry caterpillar.

4. On Monday he _____ through one apple.

5. The next day was _____ again.

6. Now he wasn't _____ any more.

7. He _____ inside for more than two weeks.

8. Then he nibbled a hole in the cocoon and pushed his _____ out.

Family Activity

Ask your family to help you make a list of long **a** and vowel **y** words. Write a sentence using two of the words.

The sound of long **a** can be spelled many ways. Read the words in the box. Listen for the sound of long **a**. Then write each word in the correct column.

able	raise	stay	space	paper	main
day	cake	flavor	rain	way	came

a-e　　　　　　**ai**　　　　　　**ay**　　　　　　**a**

_____　　_____　　_____　　_____

_____　　_____　　_____　　_____

_____　　_____　　_____　　_____

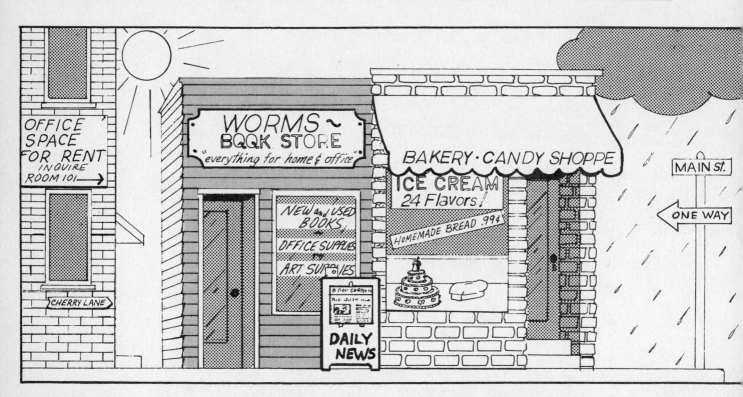

Challenge

Work with a partner to add your own words to the lists above.

_____　　_____　　_____　　_____

_____　　_____　　_____　　_____

_____　　_____　　_____　　_____

When **y** comes at the end of a one-syllable word, it usually takes the sound of long **i**. When it comes at the end of a word with more than one syllable, it usually has the sound of long **e**.

Play tic-tac-toe. Listen for the sound of **y**. Draw a line through three words in a row that have the same vowel sound. Go across, down, or corner to corner.

Listen for the sound of long **i**.

cry	yarn	jelly
sky	bunny	yard
fly	yo-yo	puppy

Listen for the sound of long **e**.

yam	buy	city
dry	baby	spy
money	fry	yak

Now make your own tic-tac-toe game. Choose words that have the sound of long **i** or long **e**. Be sure to put three words with the same vowel sound of **y** in a straight line. Let a friend play your game.

Complete each rhyme by writing a long **a** word or a word with vowel **y** on the line.

Long **a** Words

1. It takes a very hot oven to bake

   A healthy, tasty carrot _____.

2. The caterpillar will not stay.

   He'll turn into a butterfly and fly _____.

3. It's getting late.

   I cannot _____.

4. Are caterpillars ever able

   To eat a meal at a dining room _____?

Vowel **y** Words

5. Little caterpillar, don't you cry.

   Soon you'll be a butter_____.

6. Don't you think it would be _____

   If a caterpillar turned into a bunny?

7. Even though you can't yet fly,

   In your cocoon you're safe and _____.

8. Butterflies like to fly

   All around the summer _____.

Challenge

Make up your own rhyme. Use long **a** or vowel **y** words.
Leave out one word. Let a friend try to guess the answer.

Cut out the flash cards. Have a partner show you the words one at a time as you say them. Group the words together by the vowel sound heard in each word.

Time to Write ✐

Write a story about your family. See how many flash card words you can use.

gray

body

able

spy

state

money

radio

type

afraid

happy

any	way
fry	apron
very	space
myself	flavor
family	April

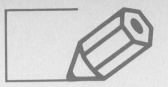

Reread "The Very Hungry Caterpillar." How would the story be different if the caterpillar were telling it?

Pretend you are the very hungry caterpillar. Tell what happens. What are you thinking? Are you surprised to find you can fly?

_____

_____

_____

_____

_____

_____

_____

_____

_____

Read each clue. Print the missing long **a** or vowel **y** word in the correct place in the puzzle.

ACROSS

2. A _____ gave the caterpillar a stomachache.
4. At the end the caterpillar becomes a _____.
7. On Monday he _____ an apple.
8. He had to _____ in the cocoon for over two weeks.

DOWN

1. The story is about a _____ hungry caterpillar.
3. The caterpillar ate so much because he was _____.
5. When he first hatched, he was _____.
6. He ate six oranges on _____.

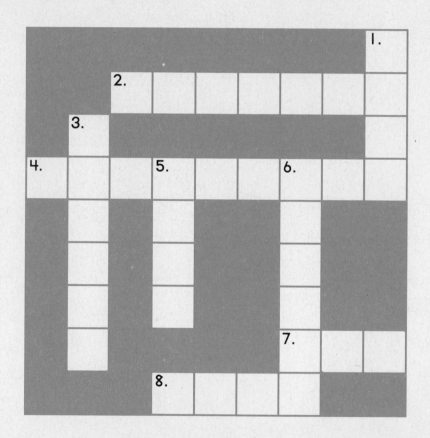

Challenge

Fuzzy! Hungry! Write some other words that describe a caterpillar.

_____

_____

_____

Say the name of each picture. Fill in the circle under the word that has the same vowel sound.

1.

sang	star	save	pat
○	○	○	○

2.

cry	many	yell	yes
○	○	○	○

3.

had	hat	camp	shade
○	○	○	○

4.

myself	your	really	yard
○	○	○	○

5.

early	shy	pretty	happy
○	○	○	○

6.

near	flat	day	drop
○	○	○	○

7.

every	yet	try	buy
○	○	○	○

Read each sentence that has been started for you. Then fill in the circle under the word that completes the sentence.

1. The _____ learned to walk.

| baby | bay | year | silly |
| O | O | O | O |

2. Remi got a letter in the _____.

| map | mail | small | date |
| O | O | O | O |

3. Did you _____ a dime for that drink?

| park | say | rang | pay |
| O | O | O | O |

4. How _____ is this desert?

| drip | my | really | dry |
| O | O | O | O |

5. The _____ has many tall buildings.

| city | sky | yard | yell |
| O | O | O | O |

6. Carol will _____ on the smooth ice.

| skate | slap | flash | gate |
| O | O | O | O |

7. My birthday comes in the month of _____.

| happy | July | very | young |
| O | O | O | O |

8. Dad put on an _____ before he started the grill.

| hat | apron | spark | April |
| O | O | O | O |

Laughing Time

—William Jay Smith

It was laughing time, and the tall Giraffe
Lifted his head, and began to laugh:

Ha!Ha!   Ha!Ha!

And the Chimpanzee on the ginkgo tree
Swung merrily down with a *Tee Hee Hee:*

Hee!Hee!   Hee!Hee!

"It's certainly not against the law!"
Croaked Justice Crow with a loud guffaw:

Haw!Haw!   Haw!Haw!

The dancing Bear who could never say "No"
Waltzed up and down on the tip of his toe:

Ho!Ho!   Ho!Ho!

The Donkey daintily took his paw,
And around they went: Hee-Haw! Hee-Haw!

Hee-Haw!   Hee-Haw!

The Moon had to smile as it started to climb;
All over the world it was laughing time!

Ho!Ho!   Ho!Ho!   Hee-Haw!   Hee-Haw!
Hee!Hee!   Hee!Hee!   Ha!Ha!   Ha!Ha!

Ha! Ha! Ho! Ho! Hee! Hee!
When is it "laughing time" for you? On the lines below, list things that make you laugh.

_____

_____

_____

_____

_____

_____

_____

_____

_____

_____

_____

_____

_____

At the Library 📖

Read these funny books.

Let's Marry Said the Cherry and Other Nonsense Poems
by N.M. Bodecker

The Man Who Kept House by Kathleen and Michael Hague

Read the poem. Some of the words are missing. Fill in the missing words so the poem makes sense.

1. It was laughing time, and the tall _____

2. Lifted his head and _____ to laugh.

3. And the Chimpanzee on the _____ tree

4. _____ merrily down with a Tee Hee Hee.

5. "It's _____ not _____ the law!"

6. Croaked _____ Crow with a loud _____.

7. The _____ bear who _____ never say "No"

8. Waltzed up and down on the tip of his toe.

Family Activity

Look through an old newspaper or magazine for words that have the sounds of **c** and **g**. Cut out the words and make a collage.

Hard and Soft c	The consonant **c** has two sounds. The hard sound of **c** is like **k**, as in *can*. The soft sound of **c** is like **s**, as in *dance*. Read the two columns of words below. Use words from both columns to make up silly sentences. The first one has been done for you.

Hard c	Soft c
cage	raced
car	pranced
caught	danced
camped	mice
cake	cereal
cactus	ceiling

1. The car raced on the ceiling. _____

2. _____

3. _____

4. _____

5. _____

6. _____

Hard and Soft c

Circus animals do funny tricks that make us laugh. Then, they go backstage to eat and rest.

Help **Carl** the laughing **camel** find his **cage** by following the sound of hard **c**.
Help **Cindy** the silly **dancing** bear find her **cement cell** by following the sound of soft **c**.

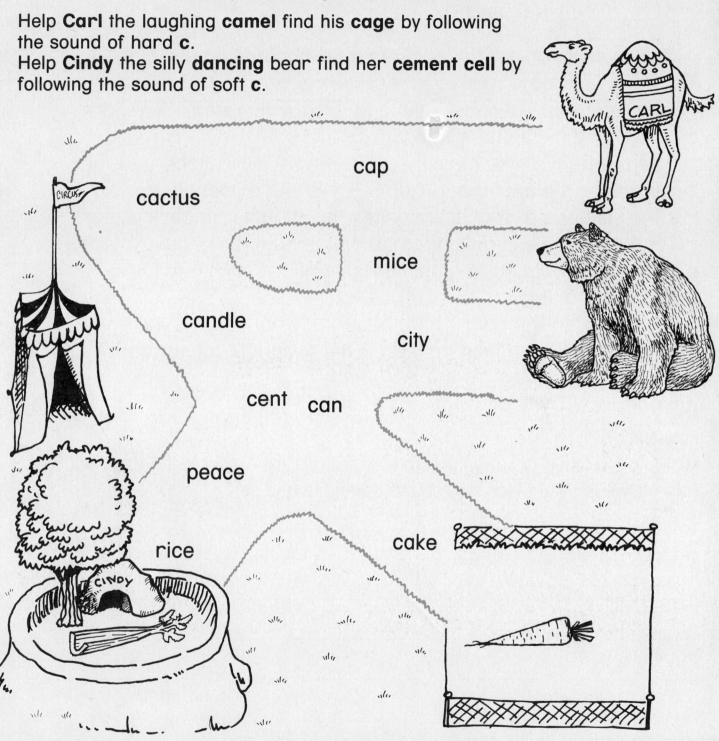

cap

cactus

mice

candle

city

cent   can

peace

rice

cake

What hard **c** word was in Carl's cage for him to eat? _____

What soft **c** word was in Cindy's? _____

The consonant **g** has two sounds. The **g** in *game* has the hard sound. The **g** in *gentle* has the soft sound. Read the fable to find out how the camel made the other animals laugh. Then reread the fable. Circle the words with the hard sound of **g**. Underline the words with the soft sound of **g**.

The animals in the jungle gave a birthday party for King Lion. The giraffe read a funny story at the party. The tiger led a game. Each animal had to try to guess the lion's age. A giant bird chirped a silly tune.

Then, a gentle little monkey danced with such grace that the other animals clapped and clapped. But the camel did not clap. He was jealous of the little monkey. He thought he could dance much better. The camel stood up on his huge hind legs. All the other animals began to giggle at the sight of such a large beast trying to do a jig.

Finally, even the camel had to laugh. "I am so silly," he said. "The monkey is the best dancer in the jungle. I cannot dance, but I tell good jokes. At the next party, I won't try to copy anyone else. I will do what I do best."

Challenge

Write a few sentences about things other animals might have done for King Lion's birthday. Use hard and soft **g** words.

_____

_____

_____

_____

_____

_____

_____

Read the words in the box. Listen for the sounds of hard and soft **g**. Then write each word in the correct column.

frog	game	gym	gift	bridge	gem
gas	change	wagon	germ	flag	village

Hard **g**

_____

_____

_____

_____

_____

Soft **g**

_____

_____

_____

_____

_____

Comic strips in the newspaper are sometimes called "funnies" because they make us laugh. Draw a "funny" in the boxes below. Use hard and soft **g** words in the balloons that show what someone is saying.

Read each joke. Write the missing hard or soft **c** or **g** word on the line.

1. Why didn't the skunk go to the store?

   He didn't have a _____.

2. Why is your nose in the middle of your face?

   Because it's the _____.

3. What did the pearl say to the diamond?

   You're a real _____.

4. What's worse than an octopus with sore feet?

   A _____ with a sore throat.

5. How can you tell when a clock is shy?

   It puts its hands in front of its _____.

6. What has four wheels and flies?

   A _____ truck.

Write a joke of your own. Use words that have the hard or soft sound of **c** or **g**. Share your joke with a classmate.

_____

_____

_____

_____

"I laughed till I cried."
"I laughed my head off."
"I laughed so hard my sides split!"

Write about a time when you just couldn't stop laughing.

_____

_____

_____

_____

_____

_____

_____

_____

_____

_____

_____

_____

_____

Find the hard and soft **c** and **g** words on the giraffe's neck. Write the words on the lines. The more words you find the closer you get to the zoo.

gemtafacemp
frogisbcapdy
ricehogymk
lcakequrgasv

_____

_____

_____

_____

_____

_____

Say the word at the beginning of each row. Then fill in the circle under the word that has the same sound of **c** or **g**.

1. gone   large ○   pig ○   giraffe ○   laugh ○

2. cent   because ○   piece ○   color ○   camp ○

3. age   bridge ○   sugar ○   frog ○   game ○

4. coat   city ○   celery ○   cap ○   prance ○

5. cake   cider ○   mice ○   trace ○   candle ○

6. gave   germ ○   page ○   wagon ○   gem ○

7. huge   flag ○   began ○   garden ○   gently ○

Read each sentence that has been started for you. Then fill in the circle under the word that completes the sentence.

1. Our _____ is the United States.

country	center	cake	peace
○	○	○	○

2. Timmy played with his little red _____.

village	danger	wagon	girl
○	○	○	○

3. Did you _____ into your old clothes?

grow	change	gift	giant
○	○	○	○

4. Use a lead _____ to write the answer.

picture	color	face	pencil
○	○	○	○

5. Put _____ in the car before a long trip.

gas	garden	goat	engine
○	○	○	○

6. Let's play basketball in the _____.

germs	gym	game	gate
○	○	○	○

7. Can you _____ this heavy bag?

carry	trace	cent	cereal
○	○	○	○

8. Peter slipped on the _____.

cold	cloud	ice	race
○	○	○	○

JohnnyAppleseed

Of Jonathan Chapman
Two things are known,
That he loved apples,
That he walked alone.

For fifty years over
Of harvest and dew,
He planted his apples
Where no apples grew.

The winds of the prairie
Might blow through his rags,
But he carried his seeds
In the best deerskin bags.

From old Ashtabula
To frontier Fort Wayne,
He planted and pruned
And he planted again.

He nested with owl,
And with bear-cub and possum,
And knew all his orchards
Root, tendril and blossom.

Why did he do it?
We do not know.
He wished that apples
Might root and grow.

—**Rosemary and Steven Vincent Benét**

Long ago, Johnny Appleseed planted his seeds. Why do you think he planted apple seeds? List your reasons inside the apples.

At the Library 📖

To find out more about Johnny Appleseed, read these books.

A Book of Americans by Rosemary and Stephen Benét

The Story of Johnny Appleseed by Aliki

Read the poem. Some of the words are missing. Fill in the missing words so the poem makes sense.

1. For fifty years over

2. Of _____ and dew,

3. He _____ his apples

4. Where no apples _____.

5. The winds of the _____

6. Might _____ _____ his rags,

7. But he carried his seeds

8. In the _____ _____ bags.

9. _____ old Ashtabula

10. To _____ Fort Wayne,

11. He planted and _____

12. And he _____ again.

13. He _____ with owl,

14. And with bear-cub and possum,

15. And knew all his orchards

16. Root, _____ and _____.

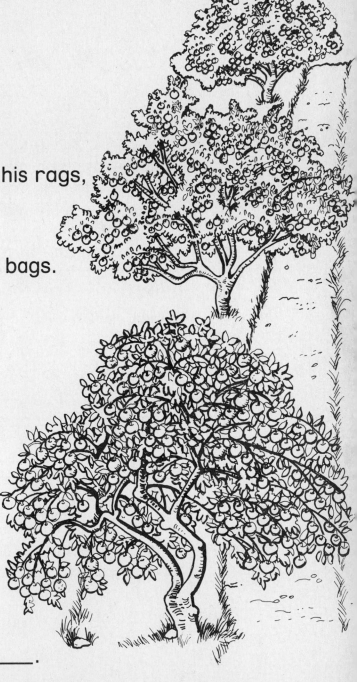

Family Activity

Sometimes two consonants appear together with no vowel between them. If their sounds blend together, they are called **blends**. In Fort Wayne, you hear the blend **rt**. Look at a map of the United States to find other places whose names have a blend. Make a list of the places you find.

Sometimes two consonants appear together with no vowel in between. If you can hear their sounds blend together, they are called blends. **Gr** is a blend in the word **green**.

This might be Johnny Appleseed's autograph.

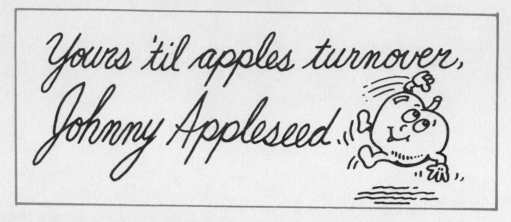

Yours 'til apples turnover,
Johnny Appleseed

When you autograph something, you write your name on it. It is fun to collect autographs. You can keep them in a special book. Sometimes people will write a saying to go with their name. Look at these pages from an autograph book. Underline the words that have **r**-blends.

I'm the friend from the country, the friend who spoiled your book by round. printing round and friend from the town, I'm

Yours 'til fruit flies,

Yours 'til
bread
boxes,

Take the road to
success...
And drive carefully.

cry,
laugh,
sign
graph!

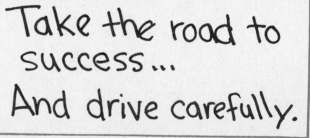

Yours 'til the
cookie crumbles.

Write a saying to go with your own autograph. Try to use words that have **r**-blends.

Read the fable. What part did the apple tree play in the story? Then reread the fable and underline all the words with l-blends, like *plant*.

A tiny ant sat under a blade of grass on the river bank. She was so thirsty that she was careless when she bent to take a drink. The little ant slipped into the swift water. She tried and tried, but the ant could not swim to shore.

Luckily, a dove resting on a branch of an apple tree saw the ant. The dove was glad to help. She plucked a leaf from the tree and dropped it close to the ant. The ant climbed on and floated safely to shore.

Soon after, the ant was out walking. She saw the dove who had saved her life. This time the dove was in trouble. A man was just about to catch her in a large net. The ant was pleased to be able to help. She quickly crawled over to the man and bit his foot as hard as she could. The man cried out in pain. The dove heard his yell and flew away to safety.

Challenge

What lesson does the story teach? Write your answer on the lines.

_____

_____

_____

_____

_____

_____

_____

S-Blends	A limerick is a funny verse that has five lines. Read this limerick to find out where a silly man grew apples.

A gardening nut from O'Hare
Grew apples so sweet in his hair.
   At a space on the beach
   He met a small peach—
Now the peach and the nut are a pear.

This limerick is about a man who likes to use his telescope at night. What do you think he sees? Read to find out if you are right.

There's a beautiful girl in the skies
Of an astronomical size.
   I gaze through my 'scope
   Each night in the hope
Of seeing the stars in her eyes.

Read the limericks again. Circle the **s**-blend words. Write the words on the lines.

_____ _____ _____

_____ _____ _____

Make up a limerick with a friend. Use an **s**-blend in your limerick.

_____

_____

_____

_____

A three-letter blend is three consonants sounded together. The words **str**eam and **thr**ow begin with three-letter blends. Answer the riddles with words that begin with a **scr**, **spl**, **spr**, **squ**, **str**, or **thr** blend.

1. My tail is bushy. I live in a tree.
Put out some nuts and you'll see me.

I am a _____.

2. I'm on your yo-yo and your kite.
I could be red, but I'm probably white.

I am the _____.

3. I'm a tiny piece of wood.
Under your skin, I don't feel good.

I am a _____.

4. Birds sing. Buds bloom.
Not the season to stay in your room.

It's _____.

5. If I should stop while you're at play,
Don't stop to talk - just run away!

I am a _____.

6. Black and red in a checkers game,
My four sides are all the same.

I am a _____.

Challenge

Write a riddle of your own. Try to use a three-letter blend in your riddle. Give it to a friend to solve.

Final Blends	Some blends come at the end of words. As you read the words, listen for the final blends. Then write a word that rhymes with each word. Use a **lf**, **mp**, **nk**, **nt**, or **st** blend at the end of the rhyming word.

1. rust _____

2. jump _____

3. hint _____

4. fast _____

5. wink _____

6. slant _____

7. skunk _____

8. fist _____

9. elf _____

10. roast _____

Say the name of each picture. Listen for the sound of **nk**, **mp**, or **st** at the end of each word. Then print two words that rhyme with the name of each picture.

_____   _____   _____

_____   _____   _____

Challenge

Write a poem using rhyming words from above.

_____

_____

_____

_____

_____

_____

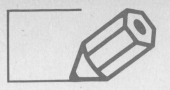

Pretend that Johnny Appleseed traveled out of the past and into the future. In fact, he is coming to your house for lunch. What foods will you serve him? Why did you choose these foods? Did you include his favorite foods? Write a short story to tell what happened when Johnny came over for lunch.

_____

_____

_____

_____

_____

_____

_____

_____

_____

_____

_____

_____

_____

_____

_____

_____

Read each clue. Write a word that has a consonant blend in the correct spaces.

ACROSS

2. apples, oranges, plums, pears
5. put a seed in the ground
6. apple blossoms have a sweet odor or ____

DOWN

1. color of an apple tree's leaves
3. apples grow on a ____
4. burst into flower

How many **l** blends are in this puzzle? _____
Use the words that have **r** blends in one sentence.

_____

Say the name of each picture. Fill in the circle under the word that has the same consonant blend.

1.

snow	small	some	mile
○	○	○	○

2.

clay	cent	sky	crow
○	○	○	○

3.

blame	back	lamp	bird
○	○	○	○

4.

fast	strike	stop	try
○	○	○	○

5.

smell	talk	mint	mind
○	○	○	○

6.

lamp	flat	wrap	half
○	○	○	○

7.

press	please	drain	rice
○	○	○	○

Read each sentence that has been started for you. Then fill in the circle under the word that completes the sentence.

1. The _____ in the sky are fluffy.

     white   clouds   could
       ○   ○   ○

2. Bake the _____ in a hot oven.

     bread   butter   pot
       ○   ○   ○

3. Peter made tracks in the new _____.

     show   music   snow
       ○   ○   ○

4. The _____ lost its leaves in the fall.

     tree   city   part
       ○   ○   ○

5. Watch the pitcher _____ the ball.

     water   throw   time
       ○   ○   ○

6. The _____ move around the sun.

     people   lamps   planets
       ○   ○   ○

7. Did you put a _____ on the letter?

     face   stamp   paper
       ○   ○   ○

8. Be sure to _____ for the spelling test.

     study   sentence   say
       ○   ○   ○

The Nicest Gift

One of the things Carlitos and Blanco like to do best is to go with Mother to the *mercado* to buy groceries and other things for the house. The *mercado* is the marketplace. On their way, they greet good friends, because in the Barrio everyone knows everyone else.

"Buenas días, Carlitos."

"Good morning, Carlitos."

There is much to see and do at the *mercado,* and always there is the *churro* wagon parked nearby. When smoke comes from the little chimney, Carlitos knows the *churro* man inside the wagon is cooking *churros. Churros* are made of sweet dough and cooked in a large kettle of boiling oil. When they are done, they look like huge pretzels.

Looking around, Carlitos sees a bunch of colored balloons dancing in the air just a short hop from the *churro* wagon, so he knows his friend Leandro is there too. Leandro is a jolly old man. He has on a large straw hat, and to attract attention to what he has to sell, he calls out his wares as if he were singing a song:

Balones!"   "Balloons!"
Cacahuatitos!"   "Peanuts!"

—Leo Politi

CHURROS

Carlitos and Blanco like to go to the mercado. List some of the things they see in the market. Then list some of your favorite things to see and do when you go out shopping.

_____

_____

_____

_____

_____

_____

_____

_____

_____

_____

_____

_____

_____

At the Library 📖

Read more about marketplaces.

Corduroy by Don Freeman

Mr. Rabbit and the Lovely Present by Charlotte Zolotow

Read the sentences from the story. Some of the words are missing. Fill in the missing words so the sentences make sense.

1. The mercado is the marketplace. On _____ way,

   _____ greet good friends, because everyone in the

   Barrio _____ everyone else.

2. There is _____ to see and do at the mercado, and

   always _____ is the churro wagon parked nearby.

3. When smoke comes from the little _____, Carlitos
   knows the churro man inside the wagon is cooking

   _____.

4. Looking around, Carlitos sees a _____ of colored

   balloons dancing in the air just a _____ hop from
   the churro wagon.

5. He has on a large straw hat, and to attract attention to

   _____ he has to sell, he calls out his wares as if he
   were singing a song:

           "Balones!"   "Balloons!"
           "Cacahuatitos!"   "Peanuts!"

Family Activity

A consonant digraph is two consonants that together make one sound like **th**, **ch**, **sh**, and **wh**. Underline the digraphs in these "shopping" tongue twisters. Share them with your family. Try to write a tongue twister of your own. Use digraphs and silent consonants in your tongue twister.

1. Top chopstick shops stock top chopsticks.
2. Sara saw a sash shop full of showy, shiny sashes.

sh, th, wh

Two consonants that join together to make one new sound are called consonant digraphs. **Sh**, **th**, and **wh** are consonant digraphs.

Did you ever try to find a certain store in a big shopping mall? You probably had to look at a map of the mall called the directory. The first thing you had to find on the directory was the spot marked YOU ARE HERE. Then, you knew where to begin. But, the words YOU ARE HERE can sometimes be confusing as you will see in this poem.

If I were   But where
Where I   I am,
Would be,   There
Then I   I must be.
Should be   And where
Where I   I would be,
Am not.   I cannot.

Reread the poem. Underline the words in the poem that have the **sh**, **th**, or **wh** digraph. Write the words on the lines.

_____   _____

_____   _____

_____   _____

_____

Challenge

Write sentences that tell about a time when you or someone you know got lost while shopping.

_____

_____

_____

_____

ph, ch, tch

Ph, **ch**, and **tch** are also consonant digraphs. **Ph** has the sound of **f**. Complete each sentence with a word from the box.

Pharmacy	purchased	batch
photograph	trophy	exchanged
change	children	watch

1. Last Saturday, Mrs. Skinner and her _____ went shopping.

2. First, Molly _____ her size 10 jacket for a size 12.

3. Then, Sam _____ a waterproof _____ with money he had earned.

4. Sam paid for it and still had some _____ left.

5. Next, Gail stopped in the sporting goods store to pick up a _____ her team had won.

6. Gail was so proud she had a _____ taken for her album.

7. Finally, the whole family bought things they needed at a drugstore called "Phil's _____."

8. The last stop was the bakery where Mom bought a _____ of hot rolls to take home for lunch.

kn, wr, ck

While Carlitos and Blanco waited for their mother to finish shopping in the mercado, they told these funny knock, knock jokes.

1. Knock, knock. *Who's there?*
   Omar. *Omar who?*
   Omar goodness! Wrong address.

2. Knock, knock. *Who's there?*
   Pickle. *Pickle who?*
   Pickle letter from A to Z.

3. Knock, knock. *Who's there?*
   Kitcheek, kitcheek. *Kitcheek, kitcheek who?*
   Don't do that, I'm ticklish.

4. Knock, knock. *Who's there?*
   Ice pick. *Ice pick who?*
   Ice pick for the people of this country.

5. Knock, knock. *Who's there?*
   Punch. *Punch who?*
   Not me! I didn't do anything wrong.

6. Knock, knock. *Who's there?*
   Minerva. *Minerva who?*
   Minerva's a wreck from all these knock, knock jokes.

Reread the jokes. Underline the words that have the **kn-**, **wr-**, or **-ck** sound. Then write the words that have the **wr-** or **-ck** sound on the lines.

_____   _____   _____

_____   _____   _____

Challenge

Write a knock, knock joke of your own. Try to use words with the silent consonants **kn**, **wr**, and **ck**.

_____

_____

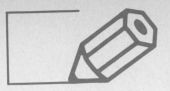

Carlitos and Blanco like to go to the mercado with their mother to shop. Do you like to go shopping with your family? Where do you go? What do you see there?

Write a letter to Carlitos and Blanco. Tell them about going shopping in your neighborhood.

_____,

_____

_____

_____

_____

_____

_____

_____

_____,

_____

Write the name of the picture on the lines. The letters in the boxes will spell something you cannot buy in a store. Write the word at the bottom of the page.

1. __ __ __ __ __ __

2. __ __ __ __ __ __

3. __ __ __

4. __ __ __ __ __ __

5. __ __ __ __ __ __

6. __ __ __ __

7. __ __ __ __

8. __ __ __ __ __ __

9. __ __ __ __

__ __ __ __ __ __ __ __ __

Say the name of each picture. Fill in the circle under the word that has the same consonant digraph or silent consonant.

1.

small	see	have	shall
○	○	○	○

2.

read	window	write	song
○	○	○	○

3.

win	whistle	hide	try
○	○	○	○

4.

fun	honey	graph	past
○	○	○	○

5.

class	haste	cent	chase
○	○	○	○

6.

ditch	cattle	wait	tow
○	○	○	○

7.

need	know	kite	cake
○	○	○	○

Read each sentence that has been started for you. Then fill in the circle under the word that completes the sentence.

1. Did your key fit the _____ ?

lock	shoe	camp	sock
○	○	○	○

2. The _____ sailed across the ocean.

scarf	days	ship	chair
○	○	○	○

3. Turn the _____ on the door to the right.

knob	needle	broken	knee
○	○	○	○

4. We heard _____ during the storm.

talk	thunder	lamp	than
○	○	○	○

5. Mom put the bracelet on her _____ .

wax	want	wrist	write
○	○	○	○

6. Bread is made from _____ .

wheat	sandwich	work	whale
○	○	○	○

7. The _____ played at recess.

children	circus	climb	batch
○	○	○	○

8. Joey learned the _____ in nursery school.

page	alphabet	paper	phone
○	○	○	○

 January

The days are short,
    The sun a spark
Hung thin between
    The dark and dark.

Fat snowy footsteps
    Track the floor.
Milk bottles burst
    Outside the door.

The river is
    A frozen place
Held still beneath
    The trees of lace.

The sky is low.
    The wind is gray.
The radiator
    Purrs all day.

—John Updike

Snow and ice,
Can be nice!

Not everyone lives in a place that has a cold, snowy January. What is this month like where you live? On the first line, write the name of the state you live in. Then list words that best describe what January is like in your home town.

_____

_____

_____

_____

_____

_____

_____

_____

_____

_____

_____

_____

At the Library

Try these winter stories.
Alfalfa Hill by Peter Parnall

Bear's Winter House by John Yeoman

Read the poem. Some of the words are missing. Fill in the missing words so the poem makes sense.

1. The days are _____,

2.   The sun a _____

3. Hung thin between

4.   The _____ and _____.

5. Fat snowy footsteps

6.   Track the _____.

7. Milk bottles _____

8.   Outside the _____.

9. The _____ is

10.   A frozen place

11. Held still beneath

12.   The trees of lace.

13. The sky is low.

14.   The wind is gray.

15. The _____

16.   _____ all day.

Family Activity

What other months of the year have the sound of **or**, **ar**, **ur**, or **er**?
Make a list and write a short poem about one of these months.

Say the name of each picture. Listen for the sound of **ar**. Then print three words that rhyme with the name of each picture.

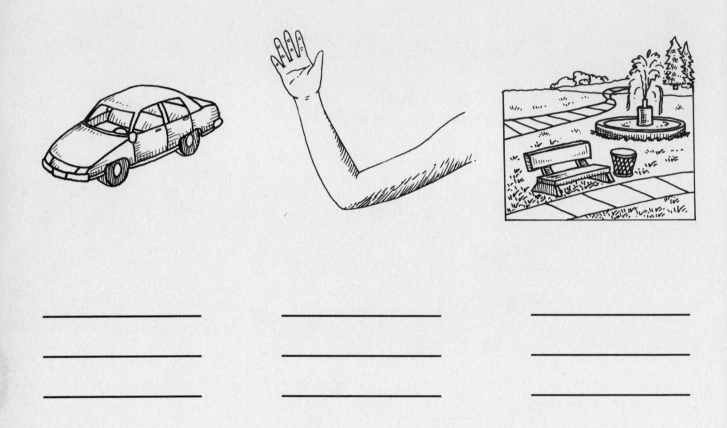

_____	_____	_____
_____	_____	_____
_____	_____	_____

Read each sentence. Write a rhyming word on the line to complete the sentence.

1. In the car we drove very _____.

2. Are you ready to start the next _____?

3. Mom will darn the socks with some _____.

4. It is not hard to make a birthday _____.

5. If you turn out the light, my dog will bark in the _____.

Read the words in the box. Listen for the sounds of **ar**, **are**, and **air**. Write each word in the correct column.

hair	barn	pair
care	square	yard
fair	share	cart
star	chair	stare

ar   **are**   **air**

_____   _____   _____

_____   _____   _____

_____   _____   _____

_____   _____   _____

Use words from the box to write a short story.

_____

_____

_____

_____

_____

_____

_____

Challenge

Draw a large square. Inside the square write words that have the sound of **are**. Then draw a big star. Fill your star with words that have the sound of **ar**.

Read the fable. Circle the **or** words. Then write the words on the lines.

One day a Hare was making fun of a slow Tortoise. As the story goes, the Tortoise challenged the Hare to a race.

The Hare ran so fast and got so far ahead, that he decided to take a short nap. While the hare slept, the Tortoise plodded on and on and reached the finish line before the Hare.

When the Hare awoke he raced to the finish, but the Tortoise was waiting for him with a smile on his face.

This was one race the Hare would not forget.

1. _____ 2. _____ 3. _____

4. _____ 5. _____ 6. _____

A moral is a lesson the fable teaches. What do you think the moral of this story is? Write your answer on the lines.

_____

_____

_____

Challenge

On another sheet of paper, rewrite the fable so that the Hare wins the race. What is the moral of your story?

Unscramble the words under each sentence. Write them in order on the lines. Listen for the sound of **er**.

1. I wonder what you do _____?
   the   winter   in

2. When you're out in the cold do you _____?
   shiver   over   all

3. Can you make a snowman with your

   sister _____?
   little   brother   or

4. Do you like to gobble up a _____?
   dinner   nice   hot

5. Did you ever catch a cold and have to stay

   home until _____?
   you   better   felt

6. Do you wear _____ to keep your feet warm?
   fuzzy   slippers   big

7. Do your _____ make you put on your hat,
   father   mother   and

   scarf, and mittens before you leave the house?

8. Or would you rather just stay in bed

   and hide _____?
   covers   the   under

Help the girl find her way to the birthday party by following the sound of **ir**. Help the nurse find his way to work by following the sound of **ur**. Use the words in the box to label the pictures as you complete the maze.

skirt	circus	purse	turkey	shirt
turtle	bird	church	circle	spur

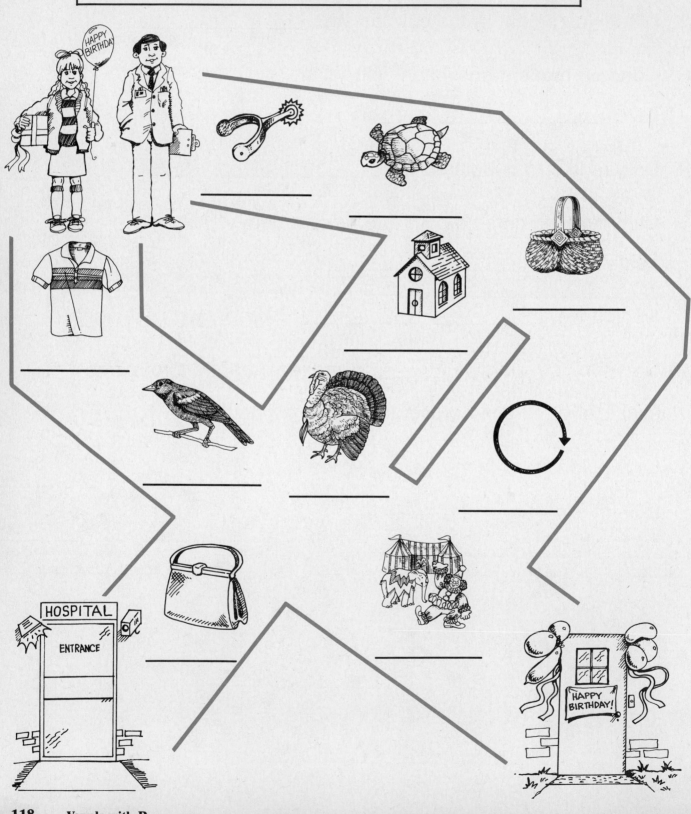

HAPPY BIRTHDAY

HOSPITAL
ENTRANCE

HAPPY BIRTHDAY!

John Updike wrote about January. Choose a month you like the best or the least. Write your own poem about that month. Is it March when spring comes? Or July when the days are warm and lazy? Is it your birthday month?

Read each clue. Write the correct word in the puzzle. The letters **ar**, **are**, **air**, **or**, **er**, **ir**, and **ur** will help you. Then use the circled letters to solve the riddle.

ACROSS
1. a house for animals
2. the color of a plum
3. something you toot
5. something that turns to ice when it's cold
7. to look at for a long time

DOWN
1. the day you were born
2. a set of two
4. a person who takes care of the sick
6. something you see in the street

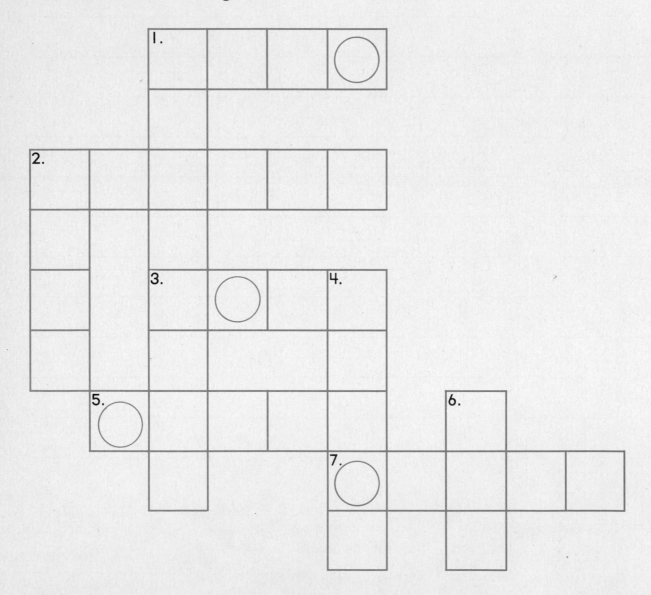

What can fall down and never get hurt? _____

Read each sentence that has been started for you. Then fill in the circle under the word that completes the sentence.

1. We saw a clown at the _____.

door	circus	river	circle
○	○	○	○

2. A _____ has a hard shell.

turtle	far	stare	turkey
○	○	○	○

3. Ted's hair is very _____.

skirt	short	nurse	over
○	○	○	○

4. The _____ was next to the table.

care	for	yard	chair
○	○	○	○

5. You can read a _____ from the book.

water	story	star	purse
○	○	○	○

6. Jane's _____ is a teacher.

cart	purple	father	girl
○	○	○	○

7. Tom broke his _____ at camp.

arm	yarn	before	fair
○	○	○	○

8. I got a new _____ for my birthday.

share	covers	purrs	shirt
○	○	○	○

Read each sentence that has been started for you. Then fill in the circle under the word that completes the sentence.

1. Mark has a big _____ in the school play.

fork	part	burst	farm
○	○	○	○

2. I wrote a _____ to my grandma.

ever	porch	curl	letter
○	○	○	○

3. Don't _____ to do your homework.

pair	brother	hurt	forget
○	○	○	○

4. The fox has a thick coat of _____.

dirt	fur	herd	cord
○	○	○	○

5. Do you take good _____ of your pets?

care	turn	better	hare
○	○	○	○

6. Bob will _____ the cake mix.

first	dinner	stir	curb
○	○	○	○

7. Do you think this test was _____?

horn	bird	hard	winter
○	○	○	○

122   **Vowels with R**

There's an Alligator under My Bed

There used to be an alligator under my bed.

When it was time to go to sleep, I had to be very careful because I knew he was there. But whenever I looked, he hid . . . or something. So I'd call Mom and Dad. But they never saw it.

It was up to me. I just had to do something about that alligator. So I went to the kitchen to get some alligator bait. I filled a paper bag full of things alligators like to eat. I put a peanut butter sandwich, some fruit, and the last piece of pie in the garage. I put cookies down the hall.

I left fresh vegetables on the stairs. I put soda and some candy next to my bed. Then I watched and waited. Sure enough, out he came to get something to eat. Then I hid in the hall closet. I followed him down the stairs. I followed him down the hall. When he crawled into the garage, I slammed the door and locked it. Then I went to bed. There wasn't even any mess to clean up.

Now that there is an alligator in the garage, I wonder if my dad will have trouble getting in his car tomorrow morning. I'll just leave him a note.

—Mercer Mayer

Draw a picture of a scary creature that might live under your bed. Scare your friends with your picture.

At the Library

Would you like to read more about how to handle scary creatures? Try these books.

Harry and the Terrible Whatzit by Dick Gackenbach

Where the Wild Things Are by Maurice Sendak

Diphthongs
oo, ew, au,
aw, and ea

Read the sentences from the story. Some of the words are missing. Fill in the missing words so the story makes sense.

1. I had to be careful _____ I _____ he was there.

2. But whenever I _____ he hid . . . or something.

3. But they never _____ it.

4. I put _____ down the hall.

5. When he _____ into the garage, I slammed the door and locked it.

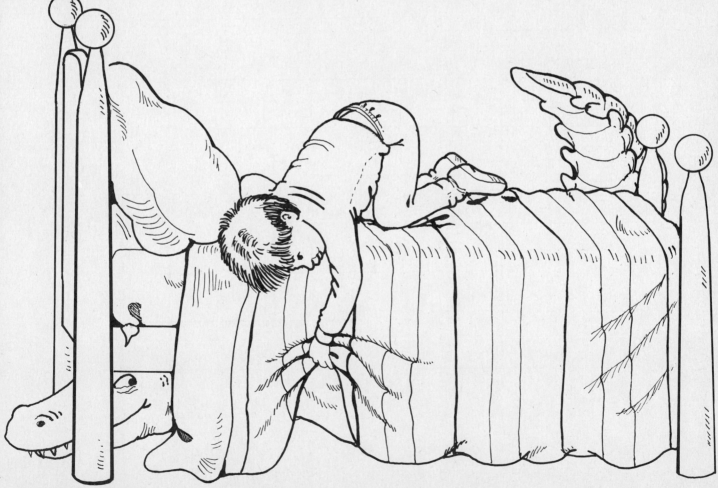

Family Activity

Check out a scary book from the library. As you read it look for words with the sounds of **oo** as in **book**, **ew**, **au**, **aw**, **oo** as in **Boo!**, or **ea** as in **head**.

The letters **ea** may stand for the vowel sound you hear in the words <u>head</u> and <u>bread</u>. Read each sentence. Write the **ea** word that completes the sentence in the puzzle. Then use the circled letters to solve the riddle at the bottom of the page.

ACROSS

2. Dad made eggs for _____.
3. There was a _____ under the bird's nest.
6. The _____ report said it was going to rain.
7. The eagle _____ its wings.
8. Your _____ sits on your shoulders.

DOWN

1. I found a _____ hidden in the attic.
4. Are you _____ for the big race?
5. They bought a loaf of _____ at the store.

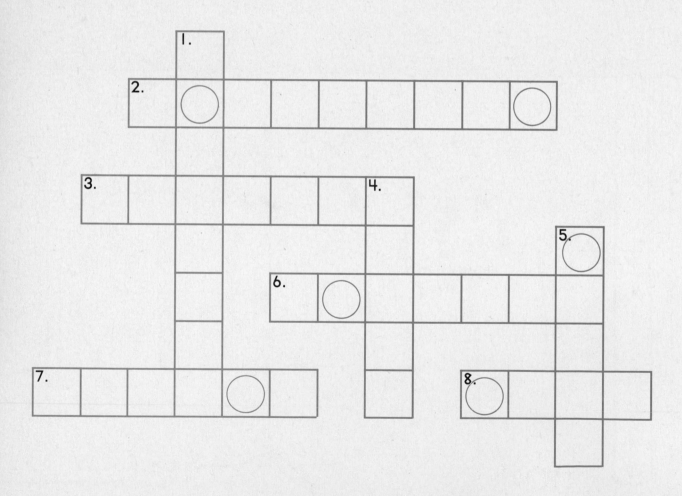

The faster you run the harder I am to catch. What am I?

Your ____ ____ ____ ____ ____ ____

Cut out the flash cards. Take turns with a partner using each word in a sentence.

Time to Write

Write a short story about something funny that happened at school.

look	soon
foot	school
took	noon
stood	room
book	cool

food	cook
pool	good
loose	shook
balloon	wood
spoon	roof

Read the fable. Circle the words that have the diphthong **ew**. Then write these words on the lines.

One spring day a hungry Rooster was scratching for food in the dirt. Suddenly his claws dug into something hard, and there on the ground was a new sparkling jewel.

The Rooster chewed on the jewel, but of course this treasure was no meal for a rooster. The Rooster had no purpose for the jewel. "For I would rather have one kernel of corn than all the jewels in the world," said the Rooster. So the Rooster threw the jewel back into the dirt and flew away.

_____ _____ _____

_____ _____

What is a treasure? When is a treasure not a treasure?

_____

_____

_____

_____

_____

_____

Diphthong aw	Say the name of each picture. Listen for the sound of **aw**. Then write three words that rhyme with the name of each picture.

saw   fawn

_____   _____

_____   _____

_____   _____

Read the **aw** words in the box. Then write a sentence using each word.

awful	draw	crawl
paws		hawk

1. _____

2. _____

3. _____

4. _____

5. _____

Read each word and listen for the sound of **au**. Write the correct word on the line to complete each sentence.

1. I turned on the _____ to get a drink of water.

2. Robin's birthday is in the month of _____.

3. The _____ has written many books about dogs.

4. The _____ wind blew through the colored leaves.

5. Tina _____ the football and scored a touchdown.

6. At the end of a sentence, you should _____.

7. Andy didn't go to the party _____ he was sick.

8. We will _____ the rocket into outer space.

Challenge

Write your own sentences using words that have the sound of **au**.

Diphthongs
ea, oo, ew,
aw, and au

Review the sounds of **ea**, **oo**, **ew**, **aw**, and **au** by unscrambling the words under each sentence. Write them in order on the line. Read the whole sentence. Does your sentence make sense?

1. I lay in the dark and _____ .
   all   shook   over

2. _____ a monster was under my bed.
   knew   I   just

3. I couldn't get that thought out _____ .
   my   head   of

4. If I climbed out of bed, would it _____ ?
   crawl   me   after

5. Bravely, I stuck my head down _____ .
   "Boo"   yelled   and

6. I guess I scared it, _____ jumped.
   monster   because   the

7. The monster sadly _____ goodbye.
   his   waved   paw

8. "Come back!" I said. "There is _____ under my bed for a monster."
   of   room   lots

Challenge

Write your own scrambled sentence about something scary. Give it to a friend to unscramble.

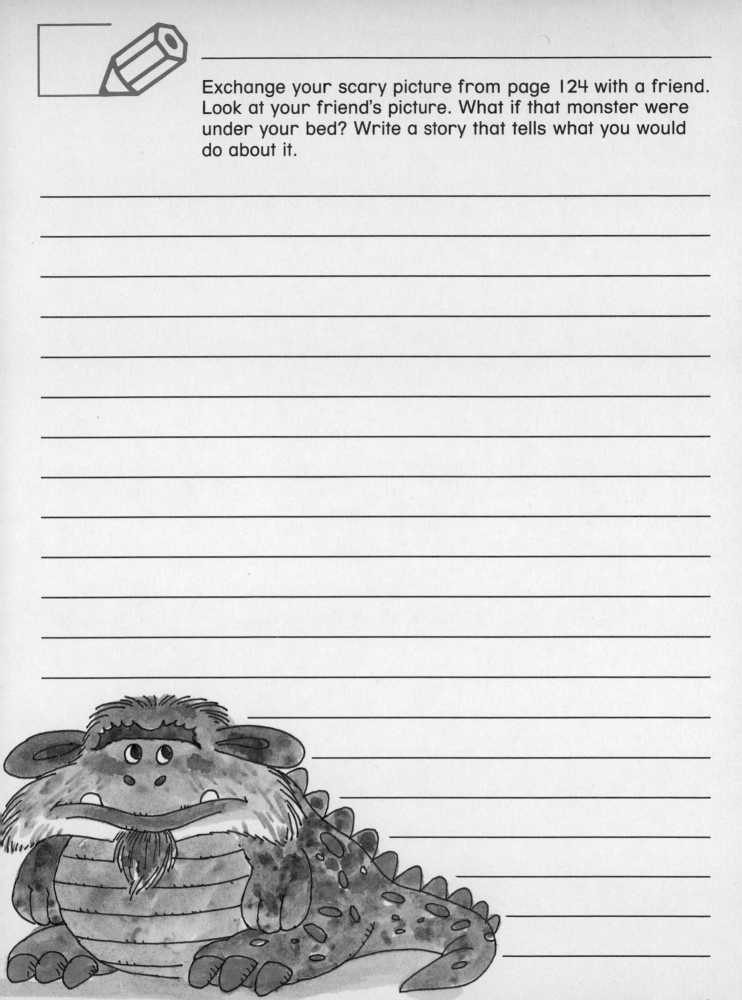

Exchange your scary picture from page 124 with a friend. Look at your friend's picture. What if that monster were under your bed? Write a story that tells what you would do about it.

_____

_____

_____

_____

_____

_____

_____

_____

_____

_____

_____

_____

_____

_____

Diphthongs
ea, oo, ew,
aw, and au

Write o͞o, o͝o, **ew**, **ea**, **au**, or **aw** in each box. Some vowel sounds have been done for you.

When you hear a word with the sound of o͞o, o͝o, **ew**, **ea**, **au**, or **aw**, write it under the correct letters. When you have five in a row, say "Bingo!"

	aw			ea
ew				
		FREE SPACE	au	
				o͝o
	o͞o			

Read each sentence that has been started for you.
Then fill in the circle under the word that completes
the sentence.

1. My mother was reading a cook _____.

   boot   hood   book   food
   ○   ○   ○   ○

2. The robin _____ on top of the roof.

   flew   pool   stew   moon
   ○   ○   ○   ○

3. Mrs. Pyle's class eats lunch at _____.

   moon   noon   blew   loose
   ○   ○   ○   ○

4. The flowers _____ wild in the field.

   dew   room   grew   new
   ○   ○   ○   ○

5. In art, Mike _____ a picture of a kangaroo.

   zoo   screw   tool   drew
   ○   ○   ○   ○

6. Bill stayed after _____ to practice the play.

   school   cool   mood   knew
   ○   ○   ○   ○

7. Marcy _____ in line to buy a ticket.

   soon   stood   wood   too
   ○   ○   ○   ○

Read each sentence that has been started for you. Then fill in the circle under the word that completes the sentence.

1. Water was dripping from the _____.

   launch   jaw   faucet   thread
   ○   ○   ○   ○

2. It was hard to lift the _____ box.

   heavy   hawk   August   feather
   ○   ○   ○   ○

3. I always _____ when I get tired.

   dawn   autumn   yawn   head
   ○   ○   ○   ○

4. Are you _____ to go to the birthday party?

   weather   cause   ready   crawl
   ○   ○   ○   ○

5. Ron mowed the _____ on Saturday morning.

   laundry   sweat   law   lawn
   ○   ○   ○   ○

6. We didn't go to the zoo _____ it was raining.

   because   caught   claw   meadow
   ○   ○   ○   ○

7. Judy met her favorite _____ at the book store.

   draw   treasure   leather   author
   ○   ○   ○   ○

8. I _____ peanut butter on a slice of bread.

   hawk   spread   lead   thaw
   ○   ○   ○   ○

Fireflies

On a summer evening I looked up from dinner, through the open window to the backyard. It was growing dark. Something flickered, a moment—I looked, and it was gone. It flickered again. Fireflies!

"Please, may I go out?" Momma smiled, and Daddy nodded.

I ran from the table, down to the cellar to find a jar. "Holes," I remembered, "so they can breathe."

The screen door banged behind me. I called to my friends, "Fireflies!"

The sky was darker now. We ran like crazy, barefoot in the grass. Suddenly a voice called out above the others, "I caught one!" And it was my own. We dashed about, catching two, ten—hundreds of fireflies, thrusting them into jars, waving our hands for more.

Then someone called from my house, "It's time to come in, now," and others called from other houses and it was over.

I climbed the stairs to my room. In the dark I watched the fireflies from my bed. They blinked off and on, but it was not the same. The fireflies beat their wings against the glass and fell to the bottom, and lay there. The light in the jar turned yellow, like a flashlight left on too long. And the light grew dimmer, green, like moonlight under water.

I flung off the covers. I went to the window, opened the jar, and aimed at the stars. "Fly!" And the fireflies poured out into the night. Fireflies! Blinking on, blinking off, dipping low, soaring high above my head, making circles around the moon, like stars dancing.

—Julie Brinckloe

It's fun to chase fireflies on warm summer nights. One thing that makes chasing fireflies special is that they only come out at certain times of the year.

What are some other special things you can only do during certain times of the year? Write some of your favorites on the lines below.

_____

_____

_____

_____

_____

_____

_____

_____

_____

_____

_____

_____

_____

At the Library 📖

Fireflies are one kind of insect. Read about other insects in these books.

The Very Busy Spider by Eric Carle

Why Mosquitoes Buzz in People's Ears: A West African Tale by Verna Aardema

Read the sentences from the story. Some of the words are missing. Fill in the missing words so the sentences make sense.

1. "Please, may I go _____?"

2. I ran from the table, _____ to the cellar to find a jar.

3. The sky was darker _____.

4. Suddenly a _____ called out above the others, "I caught one!"

5. We dashed _____, catching two, ten—hundreds of fireflies.

6. Then someone called from my _____,

   "It's time to come in, _____."

7. And the fireflies poured _____ into the night.

8. Blinking on, blinking off, dipping low, soaring high above my

   head, making circles _____ the moon, like stars dancing.

Family Activity

Ou, **oi**, **ow**, and **oy** are more vowel diphthongs. You hear these sounds in words like **couch**, **coins**, **flowers**, and **toys**. Write the names of others things in your house that have these vowel sounds.

Read the story. Circle the words that have the sound of **ou**. Then write the words on the lines.

Kangaroos are animals that live only in Australia. They have a small head that looks like a deer's. Kangaroos have a pointed snout, and big ears that stand straight up. Kangaroos use their powerful hind legs to hop. During the summer, many kangaroos rest during the day and search for food at night.

A baby kangaroo, called a "joey," can be found in its mother's pouch. The baby kangaroo travels around in the pouch and peaks its head outside. The pouch makes a good house for the joey until it is older and can take care of itself.

_____ _____ _____

_____ _____ _____

A pouch makes a good house for a baby kangaroo. A baby mouse's house may be up in the mountains, out in the woods, over in a field, or even in your house. Write a short story about a baby mouse.

_____

_____

_____

_____

_____

_____

_____

_____

_____

Say the name of the picture. Listen for the sound of **oi**.
Trace the letters **oi** in each word. Then answer the
questions at the bottom of the page.

| coins | oil | point |
| soil | boil | joint |

1. What are some things that can make n**oi**se? _____,

_____, and _____

2. What can you do with your v**oi**ce? _____,

_____, and _____

3. What are some things that sp**oi**l? _____,

_____, and _____

Diphthong ow	Say the name of each picture. Listen for the sound of **ow**. Then write three words on the lines that rhyme with the picture.

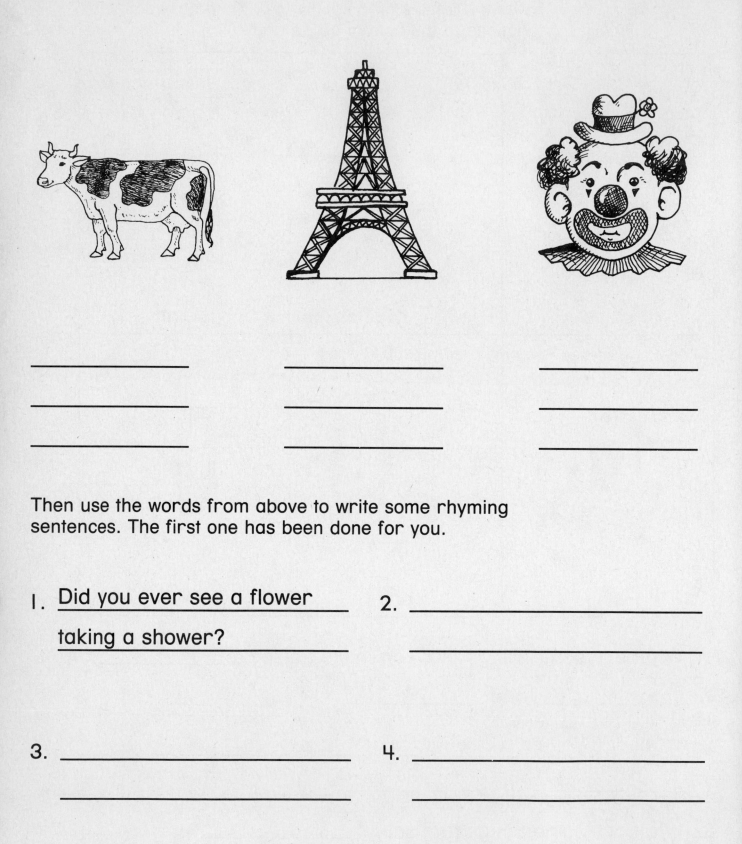

Then use the words from above to write some rhyming sentences. The first one has been done for you.

1. <u>Did you ever see a flower</u>

   <u>taking a shower?</u>

2. _____

   _____

3. _____

   _____

4. _____

   _____

Read the story. Circle the words that have the sound of **oy**. Write them on the lines.

Anne and Joyce were best friends. They lived next door to each other. They were both in Mrs. Floyd's class at school. Both girls had annoying little brothers. Anne and Joyce enjoyed doing everything together.

One day a new girl came to Mrs. Floyd's class. Her name was Jessica. Mrs. Floyd asked the boys and girls to make Jessica feel welcome. So Leroy showed her where to put her books. Troy took her to meet Soybean, the class gerbil. Then Joyce shared her toy with Jessica at recess.

Anne was worried. She felt left out. Joyce was her best friend, but she and Jessica were playing together now. Had Anne lost her most loyal friend?

_____ _____ _____ _____

_____ _____ _____ _____

_____ _____

Challenge

How can the girls solve their problem? Write your own ending for the story on the lines below. Use some of the **oy** words from the story.

_____

_____

_____

_____

_____

_____

Read each sentence. Circle the word that completes the sentence. Write the word on the line.

1. Some animals are up and _____ during the night.

house
about
soil

2. They must _____ the moonlit evenings.

enjoy
boys
voice

3. You can hear many animal _____ ring through the dark.

sounds
round
clown

4. Did you ever hear an owl _____ during the night?

point
loud
howl

5. Can you hear frogs making _____ at a nearby pond?

gown
joy
noise

6. Bats flap their wings at night, but during the day they quietly hang upside _____.

brown
down
boil

7. If an animal lives under the _____, how does it know when it's daytime or when it's nighttime?

ground
cloud
coins

8. If you had a _____, when would you be up and about?

loyal
spoil
choice

The author of "Fireflies" wrote about a special time she remembers. Write a story about a special time you remember. The list you wrote on page 138 may help you get started.

_____

_____

_____

_____

_____

_____

_____

_____

_____

_____

_____

_____

Read each clue. Then write the correct word in the puzzle. The letters **ou**, **oi**, **ow**, and **oy**, will help you. Use the circled letters to answer the riddle.

ACROSS

2. opposite of girls
4. I bloom in the spring
6. a noise
8. night birds

DOWN

1. what you sing with
3. a place to live
5. things you play with
7. opposite of up

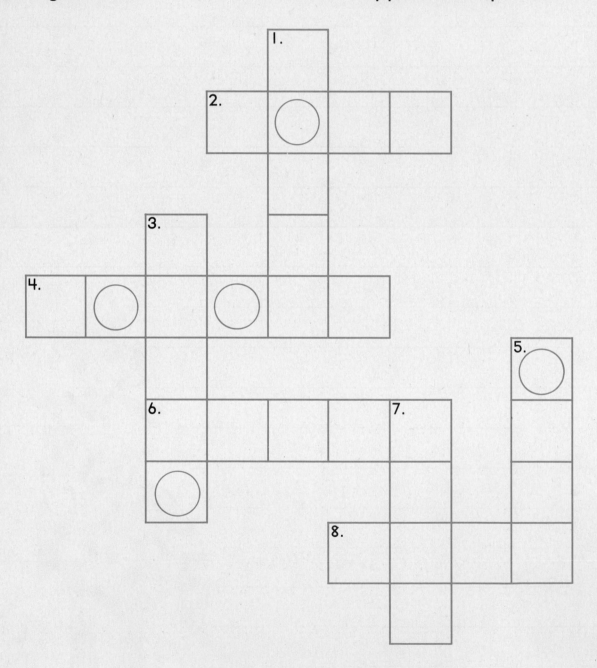

The more it dries, the wetter it gets. What is it?

a _____

Read each sentence that has been started for you. Then fill in the circle under the word that completes the sentence.

1. It was so quiet you couldn't hear a _____.

cloud	sound	out	tower
○	○	○	○

2. The queen wore a gold _____ with her gown.

crown	round	crowd	pouch
○	○	○	○

3. The plane flew over the _____ top.

mouth	down	mountain	town
○	○	○	○

4. Three pigs, two horses, and a _____ lived on the farm.

plow	count	ground	cow
○	○	○	○

5. The girls rode their bikes _____ the block.

our	around	power	vowel
○	○	○	○

6. _____ do you make chocolate ice cream?

How	Pound	House	Town
○	○	○	○

7. Ted _____ a red mitten on the playground.

owl	flower	now	found
○	○	○	○

Read each sentence that has been started for you. Then fill in the circle under the word that completes the sentence.

1. We took _____ to the children in the hospital.

   shout   toys   mouse   towels
   ○   ○   ○   ○

2. Plants need _____ to live and grow.

   oil   down   join   soil
   ○   ○   ○   ○

3. The little _____ didn't know how to swim.

   spoil   shower   boy   house
   ○   ○   ○   ○

4. I jumped when I heard the loud _____.

   noise   choice   now   round
   ○   ○   ○   ○

5. The singer had a deep _____.

   voice   coins   loud   cloud
   ○   ○   ○   ○

6. Please _____ to the picture you drew.

   joint   howl   point   pout
   ○   ○   ○   ○

7. The water was so hot that it began to _____.

   around   loyal   boil   joy
   ○   ○   ○   ○

8. Don't eat anything that has _____.

   found   crowd   counted   spoiled
   ○   ○   ○   ○

To Meet Mr. Lincoln

If I lived at the time
That Mr. Lincoln did,
And I met Mr. Lincoln
With his stovepipe lid

And his coalblack cape
And his thundercloud beard,
And worn and sad-eyed
He appeared:

"Don't worry, Mr. Lincoln,"
I'd reach up and pat his hand,
"We've got a fine president
For this land;

And the Union will be saved,
And the slaves will go free;
And you will live forever
In our nation's memory."

— Eve Merriam

Mr. Lincoln worried about the future of our country. So does the president we have now. List some things the president worries about today.

_____

_____

_____

_____

_____

_____

_____

_____

_____

At the Library 📖

Learn more about presidents of the United States.
Abraham Lincoln by Clara Ingram Judson

Franklin D. Roosevelt: Gallant President by Barbara Feinberg

Read the poem. Some of the words are missing. Fill in the missing words so the poem makes sense.

If I lived at the time

1. That Mr. _____ did,

   And I met Mr. Lincoln

2. With his _____ lid

3. And his _____ cape

4. And his _____ beard,

5. And worn and _____

   He appeared:

   "Don't worry, Mr. Lincoln,"

   I'd reach up and pat his hand,

   "We've got a fine president

   For this land;

   And the Union will be saved,

   And the slaves will go free;

6. And you will live _____

   In our nation's memory."

Family Activity

A syllable is a word or part of a word. Each syllable has one vowel sound. Ask your family to help you find a list of all our country's presidents. Name one president who has one syllable in his name. Name two presidents who have two syllables in their names. Name three presidents who have three syllables in their names.

Word Structure	A compound word is a word made up of two words like <u>campfire</u>. Read each sentence. Say the name of the pictures. Then print the compound word on the line.

1. Did the 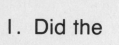 melt in the sunshine? _____

2. I found a   at the beach. _____

3. Sam ate a   for breakfast. _____

4. Our team won the   game. _____

5. On cloudy days Pam wears a   . _____

6. The puppy sleeps in the   . _____

7. My dentist gave me a new  . _____

8. In our backyard, we grew a giant  . _____

Challenge

Read each compound word. Then draw two pictures to illustrate each part of the word.

1. doorbell

2. football

3. rainbow

4. fruitcake

5. ponytail

6. clothesline

7. earring

8. campfire

Match a word from Column I to Column II to form a compound word. Then print the compound words on the lines below.

I	II		I	II
hair	day		air	fish
note	yard		down	stand
birth	cut		under	town
flash	light		gold	end
back	book		week	plane

1. _____   6. _____

2. _____   7. _____

3. _____   8. _____

4. _____   9. _____

5. _____   10. _____

Write five sentences using the compound words from your list above.

1. _____

2. _____

3. _____

4. _____

5. _____

Word Structure	A syllable is a word or part of a word. Each syllable has one vowel sound. Say the name of each picture. Listen for the number of syllables in each word. Write the words in the correct column.

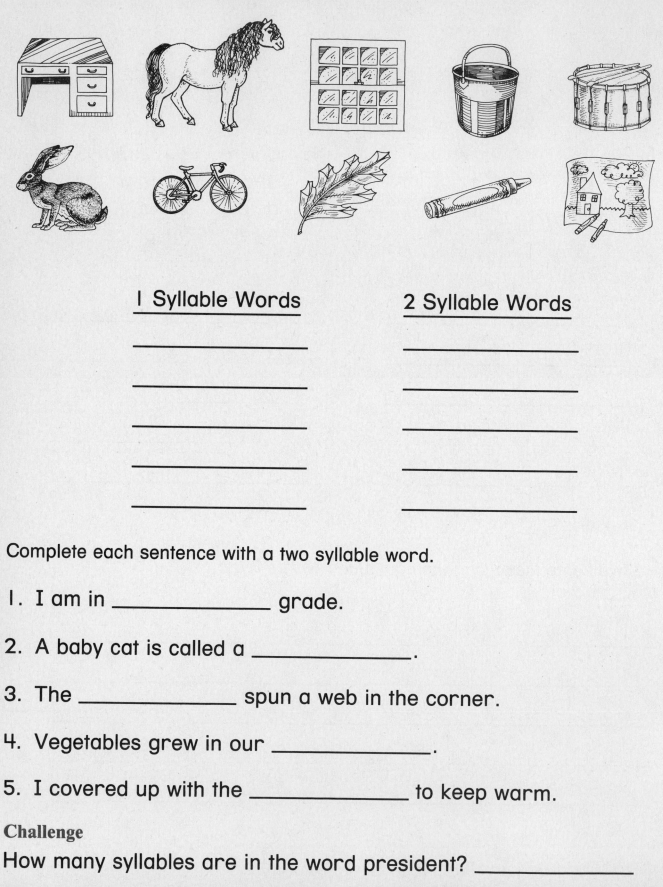

1 Syllable Words	2 Syllable Words
_____	_____
_____	_____
_____	_____
_____	_____
_____	

Complete each sentence with a two syllable word.

1. I am in _____ grade.

2. A baby cat is called a _____.

3. The _____ spun a web in the corner.

4. Vegetables grew in our _____.

5. I covered up with the _____ to keep warm.

Challenge

How many syllables are in the word president? _____

Match the beginning syllables to the ending syllables to form two syllable words. Write the words on the lines. Some ending syllables may be used more than once.

Beginning Syllables

wag
sis
bas
mus
win
med
mar
vis
ped
lem

Ending Syllables

on
ket
ic
ter
it
al

1. _____   2. _____   3. _____   4. _____

5. _____   6. _____   7. _____   8. _____

9. _____   10. _____

Add a syllable to complete each word.

1. doc _____   3. mon _____   5. cir _____

2. num _____   4. pic _____   6. sil _____

To turn a short word into a longer word you can add another syllable. Say the words in the box. Add the ending syllable to each word. Then write an equation for each real word on the line. The first one is done for you.

let
bat
cot
sit
mat
but
cut

+ ter

1. let + ter = letter
2. _____
3. _____
4. _____
5. _____
6. _____

pan
fun
thin
run
fin
win
spin

+ ner

7. _____
8. _____
9. _____
10. _____

When the first vowel sound in a word is followed by two consonants, divide the word between the two consonants. The first vowel sound will be short.

Read each word. Divide each word into two syllables. Write one syllable on each line. A hyphen (-) is used between syllables.

1. batter _____-_____

2. finger _____-_____

3. letter _____-_____

4. runner _____-_____

5. winner _____-_____

6. rabbit _____-_____

7. pepper _____-_____

8. hammer _____-_____

9. yellow _____-_____

10. pencil _____-_____

11. muffin _____-_____

12. napkin _____-_____

13. puppet _____-_____

14. button _____-_____

15. sister _____-_____

When the first vowel sound in a word is followed by a consonant, first try to divide the word before the consonant. Say the first vowel with a long sound. Your next step is to try dividing the word after the consonant. Then the first vowel has a short sound.

pī-lot   săl-ad

The words in the box are divided into syllables. Mark the vowel in the first syllable with a – if it is said with a long sound, and with a ˘ if it is said with a short sound.

de-cide	lo-cate	sol-id	me-ter
hab-it	mod-el	pro-tect	fla-vor

Write a word from the box on the line to complete each sentence.

1. Dennis made a _____ plane for his brother.

2. A _____ is longer than a yard.

3. What _____ is your ice cream?

4. I can't _____ what to buy with my dime.

5. Get in the _____ of making your bed.

6. The ice cubes were frozen _____.

7. Sue's umbrella will _____ her from the rain.

8. Did you _____ China on the map?

Use a word from the box to complete each sentence. Make sure you divide the word correctly.

seven
paper
honest
student
humor
cabin

Abraham Lincoln was born in Kentucky in 1809. He and his mother, father, and sister lived in a one-room log _____

_____ .

Abe was a good _____

_____ even though he could not go to school very often. He did not have any _____

_____ to write on or a pencil. Abe had a good sense of _____

_____ and liked to tell funny stories.

When Abe was _____

_____ his family moved to a state that did not have slaves. Abraham helped his father build a new cabin and plant a garden.

Abraham Lincoln grew to be an _____

_____ man. He was one of the great Presidents of the United States.

Challenge

What else do you know about Abraham Lincoln? Write a few sentences of your own to tell about him.

_____

_____

_____

Read the story. Circle the words that end in **le**. Then write the words on the lines.

Long ago, the wind and the sun had a battle to see who was stronger. Seeing a man with a purple cloak passing by, they decided to have a little contest. The contest was to see who was able to make the man take off his cloak first.

The wind began and blew with all his might. But the stronger he blew, the tighter the man clung to his cloak.

Next it was the sun's turn. The sun let his warm rays fall upon the traveler. Feeling the gentle warmth on his shoulders, the man sat down and took off his cloak.

1. _____

2. _____

3. _____

4. _____

5. _____

Should people be more like the wind or the sun? Write a few sentences to explain your answer.

_____

_____

_____

_____

A word is missing in each sentence. Write the correct word in the puzzle. Use words that end in the syllable **le**.

ACROSS

2. The wax from the _____ dripped on the table.
6. Tom told me a _____ and a joke.
7. Jan set the _____ for dinner.
8. An _____ is a strong bird.

DOWN

1. A piece is missing from the _____.
3. We had _____ pie for dessert.
4. Joe's _____ sister is only in first grade.
5. A tire is shaped like a _____.

Word Structure	Read each sentence. Circle the word that completes the sentence. Write the word on the line.

1. George Washington's _____ is February 22, 1732.

      mailbox
      handshake
      birthday

2. John Adams was the _____ president of the United States.

      seven
      second
      robin

3. Abraham Lincoln's face is pictured on the _____.

      silent
      bacon
      penny

4. Many _____ voted for the president.

      tiger
      candle
      people

5. Did you ever _____ Washington, D.C?

      cabin
      visit
      metal

6. The president works in the Oval _____.

      Office
      traffic
      wagon

7. The president eats _____ with many guests in the White House.

      river
      dinner
      apple

8. The president _____ all over the country.

      frozen
      never
      travels

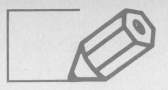

George Washington was our country's first president. He worried about the country he helped build. He worried about whether or not the country would grow strong and rich. He worried about whether the people would keep the freedom he fought to win for them. What might you say to Mr. Washington to help him worry less?

_____

_____

_____

_____

_____

_____

_____

_____

Read each president's name. Then divide each name into two syllables.

Wilson

_____-_____

Truman

_____-_____

Tyler

_____-_____

Lincoln

_____-_____

Nixon

_____-_____

Monroe

_____-_____

Carter

_____-_____

Garfield

_____-_____

Read each sentence that has been started for you. Then fill in the circle under the word that completes the sentence.

1. Ron rang the _____ to see if anyone was home.

| notebook | sunflower | doorbell | football |
| O | O | O | O |

2. We sat around the _____ to keep warm.

| oatmeal | campfire | airplane | snowman |
| O | O | O | O |

3. My umbrella blew away in the _____.

| necklace | baseball | mailbox | rainstorm |
| O | O | O | O |

4. I cleaned the tank for my _____.

| goldfish | doghouse | understand | weekend |
| O | O | O | O |

Read each word. Then fill in the circle under the word that has been correctly divided into syllables.

1.

| yell-ow | ham-mer | wi-nter | butt-on |
| O | O | O | O |

2.

| stud-ent | bac-on | pa-per | mus-ic |
| O | O | O | O |

3.

| wag-on | seco-nd | ca-bin | le-mon |
| O | O | O | O |

4.

| cand-le | circ-le | vi-sit | gen-tle |
| O | O | O | O |

Read each sentence that has been started for you. Then fill in the circle under the word that completes the sentence.

1. Tom won a gold _____ in the race.

pedal	sitter	runner	medal
○	○	○	○

2. I put my school books on the _____.

letter	desk	meat	market
○	○	○	○

3. Please pass the _____ and rolls.

purple	butter	table	window
○	○	○	○

4. The boats sailed up and down the _____.

river	crayon	basket	picnic
○	○	○	○

5. Liz forgot her _____ at the library.

lemon	little	eagle	pencil
○	○	○	○

6. Jenny wants to be a _____ when she grows up.

puppet	frozen	pilot	tulip
○	○	○	○

7. On the playground, Jerry hurt his little _____.

tiger	finger	silent	handle
○	○	○	○

Rain Sizes

Rain comes in various sizes.
Some rain is as small as a mist.
It tickles your face with surprises,
And tingles as if you'd been kissed.

Some rain is the size of a sprinkle
And doesn't put out all the sun.
You can see the drops sparkle and twinkle,
And a rainbow comes out when it's done.

Some rain is as big as a nickel
And comes with a crash and a hiss.
It comes down too heavy to tickle.
It's more like a splash than a kiss.

When it rains the right size and you're wrapped in
Your rainclothes, it's fun out of doors.
But run home before you get trapped in
The big rain that rattles and roars.

—John Ciardi

Splish! Splash! Sprinkle! It's fun to be out in the rain if "you're wrapped in your rainclothes." On the lines below, write the names of some things you like to wear on rainy days.

At the Library 📖

Would you like to read more about rain? Try these books.
Bringing the Rain to Kapiti Plain by Verna Aardema
Umbrella by Taro Yagawa

Read the poem. Some of the words are missing. Fill in the missing words so the poem makes sense.

1. Rain comes in various sizes.

2. Some rain is as small as a mist.

3. It tickles your face with surprises,

4. And tingles as if _____ been kissed.

5. Some rain is the size of a sprinkle

6. And _____ put out all the sun.

7. You can see the drops sparkle and twinkle,

8. And a rainbow comes out when _____ done.

9. Some rain is as big as a nickel

10. And comes with a crash and a hiss.

11. It comes down too heavy to tickle.

12. _____ more like a splash than a kiss.

13. When it rains the right size and _____ wrapped in

14. Your rainclothes, _____ fun out of doors.

15. But run home before you get trapped in

16. The big rain that rattles and roars.

Family Activity

Look up the word contraction in the dictionary. Write a definition for the word. Give an example of a contraction.

Contractions

A contraction is formed when two words are put together to make a shorter word. One or more letters are left out. An apostrophe is used in place of the missing letters.

I + will = I'll   you + will = you'll

Read the words in the puddles. Write the contraction for each pair of words on the line.

she + will = _____

he + will = _____

it + will = _____

we + will = _____

they + will = _____

that + will = _____

Write some silly sentences about rain. Use the contraction for each pair of words in your sentence. The first one has been done for you.

we will

1. If it keeps raining, we'll have to swim home! _____

it will

2. _____

you will

3. _____

they will

4. _____

Read the fable. Circle each contraction. Then turn the fable into a play. On each line write what the Lion or the Mouse would say. You may need to continue on another sheet of paper.

Long ago, a small mouse wasn't looking where he was going and wandered into a lion's den. The lion snatched the mouse up in his great paws. The lion hadn't eaten all day and was just about to make a meal out of him, when the mouse spoke up.

"Please don't hurt me," the mouse pleaded. "I didn't mean to disturb you. I am much too little for a great lion like you to eat."

The fierce lion looked at the little mouse and then set him free.

A few days later, the lion was hunting in the woods and fell into a trap. The lion let out a roar that filled the forest.

The little mouse heard the roar and ran quickly to the lion. "I can't get out of this net," cried the lion. The mouse's sharp teeth cut the ropes around the lion, and set him free.

Moral: One good turn deserves another.

Mouse: "Where am I?" _____

Lion: "You're in my den." _____

Mouse: _____

Lion: _____

Mouse: _____

Lion: _____

Mouse: _____

Lion: _____

Mouse: _____

Lion: _____

Mouse: _____

Lion: _____

Contractions formed with **is** and **has** look the same.

who + is = who's   it + is = it's

who + has = who's   it + has = it's

Read each pair of sentences. Circle the contractions.
Write the words the contractions stand for on the lines.

1. ____ ____   When a panda is born it's smaller than a mouse. It only weighs a few ounces.

2. ____ ____   There's an animal that does not have to lie down to go to sleep. A horse can sleep standing up.

3. ____ ____   My brother likes to read about snakes. He's learned that most snakes can go an entire year without any food.

4. ____ ____   Did you know a hippopotamus can run fast? It's been known to run faster than a person!

5. ____ ____   Here's an animal that is a great swimmer. A porcupine's quills help him float.

6. ____ ____   What's a "joey"? A joey is a baby kangaroo.

Read each sentence. Circle the contraction that completes the sentence. Write the contraction on the line. The examples at the top will help you.

I am = I'm   you are = you're   we have = we've

1. _____ watching the weather report to see if it is going to rain.

We've
I'm
I've

2. _____ dark clouds in the sky this morning.

I'm
We're
There're

3. _____ going to need your umbrella today!

You're
I've
They've

4. _____ reading about rain in our science books.

You've
I've
We're

5. _____ learned that rain helps clean the air by washing away dust.

I'm
We've
We're

6. _____ heard that it does not rain very much in the desert.

You've
I'm
You're

7. When you see raindrops, _____ different shapes and sizes.

you've
they're
we're

8. _____ seen a rainbow before, have you?

You're
I'm
I've

Contractions	Contractions formed with **had** and **would** look the same.

I + had = I'd   you + had = you'd
I + would = I'd   you + would = you'd

Read each sentence. Circle the contraction. Decide if the contraction uses the word **had** or **would**. Write the words the contraction stands for on the lines.

1. "I'd like to go on a picnic today," said Paul.   _____ _____

2. Cathy and Bob said, "We'd like to go with you."   _____ _____

3. "It'd better stop raining before you go to the park," said mother.   _____ _____

4. "Who'd like to have a picnic inside? " asked Cathy.   _____ _____

5. "That'd be a good idea," answered Bob.   _____ _____

6. "It'd be fun to spread the blanket on the floor and eat our lunches," said Paul.   _____ _____

7. Then Bob said he'd bring some games they could all play.   _____ _____

8. There'd be other sunny days for their picnic in the park.   _____ _____

Challenge

Write two sentences that use contractions with the words *had* and *would*. Give your sentences to a friend.

_____

_____

Cut out the flash cards. Work with a partner. Take turns reading the words. Then turn the words into a contraction.

Time to Write

Write five sentences using words on the front of your cards. Then write the same sentences using the contractions on the back of the cards.

I am

they will

cannot

are not

she has

what is

you are

we have

he would

you had

they'll	I'm
aren't	can't
what's	she's
we've	you're
you'd	he'd

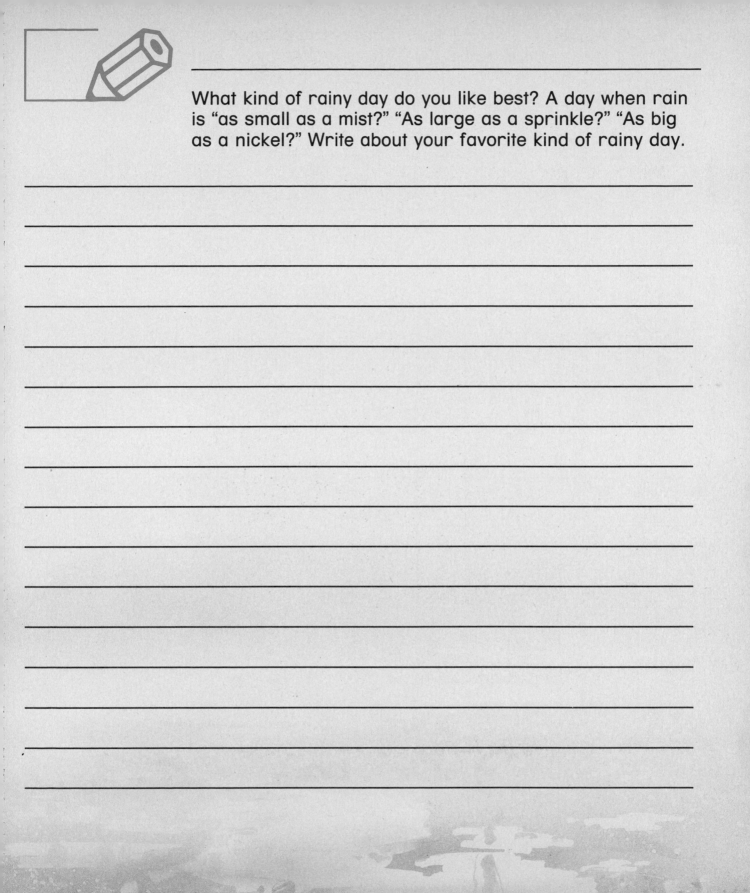

What kind of rainy day do you like best? A day when rain is "as small as a mist?" "As large as a sprinkle?" "As big as a nickel?" Write about your favorite kind of rainy day.

Read each pair of words. Write the contraction that stands for the words in the puzzle.

ACROSS
2. they are
5. do not
6. have not
7. she has

DOWN
1. we would
3. here is
4. you have
6. he will

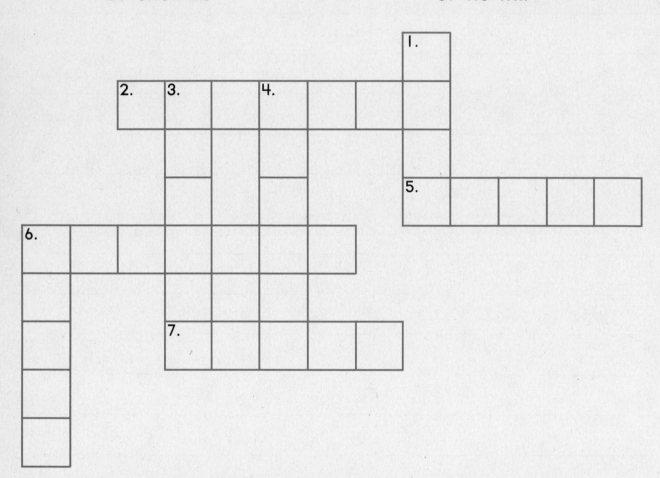

What is most useful when it's used up?
To find out, match the letters with the contractions and words.

a = is not   n = we will   b = he has
m = you are   e = we would   u = it is
l = I am   r = they had

_____ _____
isn't   we'll

_____ _____ _____ _____ _____ _____ _____ _____
it's   you're   he's   they'd   we'd   I'm   I'm   isn't

Read each contraction. Then fill in the circle under the two words the contraction stands for.

1. I've

I am ○ I are ○ I have ○ I will ○

2. don't

do not ○ does not ○ did not ○ do now ○

3. we'll

we can ○ we will ○ will not ○ he will ○

4. you'd

you not ○ you would ○ you can ○ you have ○

5. that's

this is ○ that am ○ that is ○ that was ○

6. aren't

are has ○ are had ○ were not ○ are not ○

7. they're

they are ○ they have ○ their are ○ they would ○

Read each sentence that has been started for you. Then fill in the circle under the contraction that completes the sentence.

1. _____ like to go to the game on Saturday.

That'd	We'd	She's	Don't
○	○	○	○

2. It _____ time for lunch yet.

can't	here's	isn't	she'll
○	○	○	○

3. _____ going to visit their grandma today.

They'd	Where's	They're	You've
○	○	○	○

4. _____ the last person standing in line?

Who's	We're	You'll	She'd
○	○	○	○

5. _____ going to help me bake cookies.

I've	She'd	You're	They've
○	○	○	○

6. _____ in that big pretty box?

They'll	That'll	Who'd	What's
○	○	○	○

7. _____ going to sing a song about raindrops.

I'm	I'll	He'll	He'd
○	○	○	○

8. The children _____ been to the circus.

we've	here's	haven't	it's
○	○	○	○

Good-bye Arnold!

Webster was lying in bed. He was thinking about why he hated his big brother, Arnold. There were many reasons. Arnold didn't share. And he had toys and games that Webster was not allowed to put a paw on. That night Webster had a dream that Arnold was leaving home.

The very next morning there was a phone call from Grandma. She invited Arnold to come and visit for a whole week. As soon as Arnold was out the front door, Webster ran back to their room—to Arnold's side. He tried out everything.

That night Webster climbed up to Arnold's top bunk to sleep. In the middle of the night Webster woke up. He sat up and listened. "I hear too much quiet!" he yelled, but no one heard him. It took Webster a long time to get back to sleep.

On Saturday morning Webster had to clean the whole bedroom all by himself. When he tried to make up the top bunk, the quilt fell down over the side of the bed and he couldn't pull it up. But then he had an idea. He took his quilt and pushed it under Arnold's mattress.

"Wait 'til Arnold sees my cave!" he said.

"What's this?" gasped a voice that Webster knew well. Arnold was home. "Say, that's not a bad cave," he said. "Can I come in?"

He pulled back a corner of the quilt, and Arnold climbed in. "Grandma makes good cookies," he said, "but it's too quiet at her house."

"Well," said Webster, "it's not too quiet here!"

—P.K. Roche

It's not unusual to be angry once in a while with your brother, sister, cousin, or best friend. When you finish being angry, you'll be good friends again.

Make a list of reasons for liking your brother or sister. If you don't have a brother or sister, write about a cousin or best friend. Remember the list the next time you get angry.

He is fun to be with

She helps me . . . .

_____

_____

_____

_____

_____

_____

_____

_____

_____

_____

_____

_____

At the Library

Read these books about friendship.
Ramona The Pest by Beverly Cleary

The Tenth Good Thing About Barney by Judith Viorst

Read the sentences from the story. Some of the words are missing. Fill in the missing words so the sentences make sense.

1. Webster was _____ in bed.

2. That night Webster had a dream that Arnold

   was _____ home.

3. Grandma _____ Arnold to come and visit for a whole week.

4. Webster ran back to their room—to _____ side.

5. He _____ out everything.

6. He sat up and _____.

7. He took his quilt and pushed it under _____ mattress.

8. He _____ back a corner of the quilt,

   and Arnold _____ in.

Family Activity

Plural means more than one. **Brothers** is the plural of **brother**. **Patches** is the plural of **patch**. **Bunnies** is the plural of **bunny**. What are the plurals of **sister**, **cat**, **batch**, **bush**, **pony**, and **family**?

Say the name of each picture. Notice that when there is more than one (plural), an **s**, or **es** is added to the root word. Most words form their plural by adding **s**. Words that end with **ch**, **sh**, **ss**, **z**, or **x** need **es**.

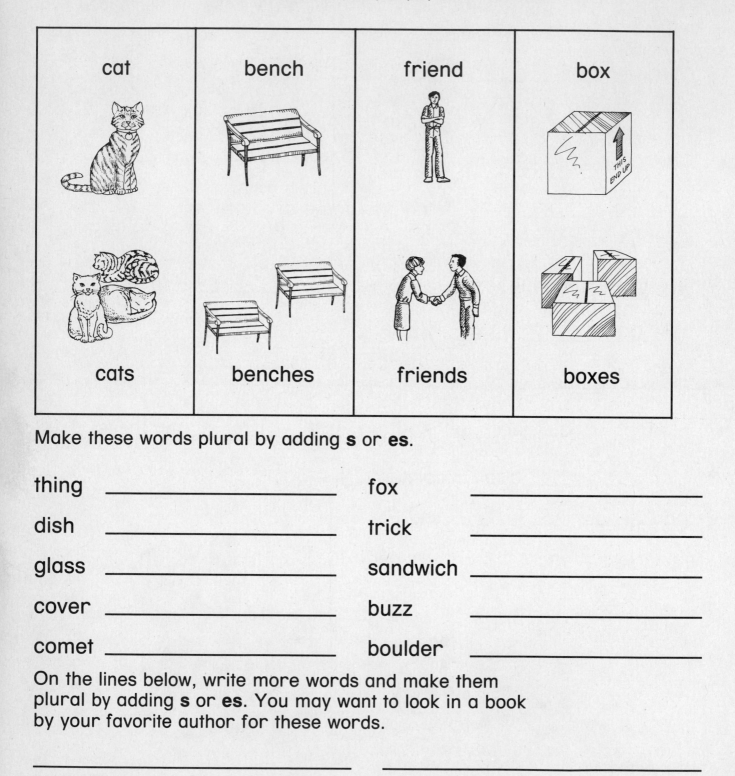

cat   bench   friend   box

cats   benches   friends   boxes

Make these words plural by adding **s** or **es**.

thing _____   fox _____

dish _____   trick _____

glass _____   sandwich _____

cover _____   buzz _____

comet _____   boulder _____

On the lines below, write more words and make them plural by adding **s** or **es**. You may want to look in a book by your favorite author for these words.

_____   _____

_____   _____

_____   _____

The plural of some words is formed by changing one or more letters in the word.

mouse – mice   goose – geese

Some words do not need spelling changes to make them plural.

moose – moose   deer – deer

Read each story problem. Write the answer on the lines.
The first one is done for you.

1. I foot   +   I foot   = __2__ __feet__

2. I mouse   +   6 mice   = ___ _____

3. Roberto had I tooth filled on Friday. He had another tooth filled on Monday. Altogether Roberto had

___ _____ filled.

4. I ox   +   I ox   = ___ _____

5. There was one child playing on the swings. Two more girls came out to swing. Now, there are

___ _____ on the swings.

6. I goose   +   9 geese   = ___ _____

7. I moose  + I moose   = ___ _____

Challenge

Now write a story problem of your own. Use words that are not made plural by adding **s** or **es**. Give your problem to a friend to solve.

Read this example.

Man is to **men** as **woman** is to **women**.

Look at the first pair of words in dark print. **man - men**
Think about how these two words are alike. **Men** means more than one man. **Men** is the plural of **man**.

How are the second pair of words alike? **Women** means more than one **woman**. **Women** is the plural of woman.

Can you tell what word finishes this sentence?

Goose is to **geese** as **mouse** is to _____.

The answer is **mice**. **Geese** is the plural of **goose** and **mice** is the plural of **mouse**.

Read each example. Think about how the words are the same. Write the last word on the line.

1. Tooth is to teeth as foot is to _____.

2. Ox is to oxen as child is to _____.

Write the two missing words on the lines.

3. Moose is to _____ as _____ is to trout.

4. Sheep is to _____ as _____ is to deer.

| Endings and Possessives | | |

You can add endings to base words to make new words.
Finish the chart by adding the endings to the base words.

Base Word	s	ed	ing
walk	walks	walked	walking
turn	_____	_____	_____
clean	_____	_____	_____
work	_____	_____	_____
stay	_____	_____	_____

Read these sentences.

We **walked** to school yesterday.
They will be **walking** to school every Friday.

Complete each sentence by adding the ending **ed** or **ing** to the word at the end of the sentence. Write the new word on the line.

1. Amy _____ over the highest boulder.   jump

2. Arnold always _____ a book in his suitcase.   pack

3. Are you _____ all the cats?   keep

4. It _____ during the night.   rain

5. The man _____ Webster out of the water.   help

6. _____ tricks can get you in trouble.   Play

7. The band will be _____ through Hannibal.   march

8. The boys _____ about Haley's comet.   dream

When a word ends in a single consonant and the vowel sound is short, double the consonant before adding ed or ing. There is no spelling change when adding s.

slip	slips	slipped	slipping
plan	plans	planned	planning
hop	hops	hopped	hopping

Read the words. Think about the rule for adding the **ed** and **ing** endings. Write the words in the correct column.

1. fit
2. clip
3. play
4. scrub
5. wait
6. wag

7. drop
8. pass
9. clean
10. shop
11. beg
12. ask

Double the final consonant before adding ed or ing

_____

_____

_____

_____

_____

_____

No spelling change

_____

_____

_____

_____

Read each sentence. Cross out the word that is not spelled correctly. Then write it correctly on the line.

1. Joging in the park is fun. _____

2. Last year it rainned for the parade. _____

3. Oh, no! I droped my glass! _____

4. Juan is peting the little puppy. _____

5. The fish are swiming around in the clear water. _____

6. Are you dreamming about being a famous writer? _____

7. I have been waitting for an hour! _____

8. Kenji shoped for a gift for his sister. _____

| Endings and Possessives | When a word ends in silent **e**, drop the **e** before adding the endings **ed** or **ing**. There is no spelling change when adding **s**. |

rescue   rescues   rescued   rescuing
escape   escapes   escaped   escaping

Read this example.

Skate is to **skated** as **like** is to **liked**.

Look at the first pair of words in dark print. **skate-skated**
Think about how the two words are alike.
Skated is the base word **skate** with the ending **ed** added.

How are the second pair of words alike? **like-liked**
Liked is the base word **like** with the ending **ed** added.

Read each example. Think about how the words are alike.
Write the missing word on the line.

1. Sleep is to sleeping as leap is to _____.

2. Hope is to hoping as drive is to _____.

3. Joke is to joking as pile is to _____.

4. Smile is to smiled as bake is to _____.

5. Camp is to camping as eat is to _____.

Challenge

6. Trace is to _____ as _____ is to pleases.

7. Vote is to _____ as _____ is to closing.

The **ed** ending tells you that something has already happened.

I **skated** until four o'clock yesterday.

Read the story to see the trouble a brother and sister got in together. Then circle the words with the **ed** ending.

Archie and Amy played tricks all the time. They always hoped they wouldn't get caught, but they always did.

One Saturday they sprinkled pepper on an apple pie. They knew Uncle Tony loved apple pie. When he came to visit, they gave him a big piece. Uncle Tony took a bite. Archie and Amy laughed when Uncle Tony sneezed and coughed.

Then they escaped by hiding in the closet. They knew Uncle Tony would soon think of a trick to pay them back. They decided they would never try that trick again.

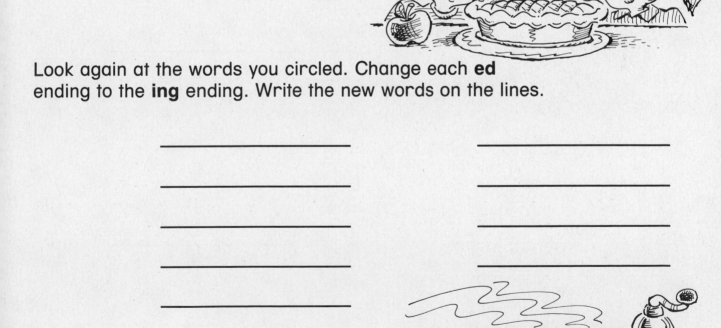

Look again at the words you circled. Change each **ed** ending to the **ing** ending. Write the new words on the lines.

_____   _____

_____   _____

_____   _____

_____   _____

_____

Challenge

Has anyone ever played a trick on you?
Write a story about it.

Endings and Possessives

When a word ends in **y** with a consonant before it, change the **y** to **i** before adding **es** or **ed**. There is no spelling change when adding **ing**.

berry   berries
cry   cries   cried   crying

Read each word. Change the word by adding the new ending. Then write the word on the line.

1. pony   _____ (s)

2. bury   _____ (ing)

3. empty   _____ (ed)

4. party   _____ (s)

5. key   _____ (s)

6. deny   _____ (ing)

7. dry   _____ (ing)

8. fry   _____ (ed)

Read each sentence. If all the words are spelled correctly, write "No change" on the line. If a word is misspelled, cross it out and write it correctly on the line. The first one is done for you.

1. Webster always ~~copyed~~ his big brother Arnold.   _____copied_____

2. When Arnold went to Grandma's house, Webster staied home.   _____

3. Webster tryed out all Arnold's toys.   _____

4. He emptied all the shelves.   _____

5. He was still playing when Arnold came home.   _____

6. "I told you not to play with my toys," he cryed.   _____

7. Webster spied on Arnold playing alone with all his toys.   _____

8. "Come in," Arnold replyed. "It's more fun to play together.   _____

Challenge

Write a sentence with a misspelled word. Challenge a friend to find and correct it.

Endings and Possessives	The ending **er** may be used to compare two things. The ending **est** may be used to compare more than two things.

tall   taller   tallest

In each box, match the picture to the correct word.
Write the correct letter on the line.

1.		2.	
a. ____ short		a. ____ slow	
b. ____ shorter		b. ____ slower	
c. ____ shortest		c. ____ slowest	
3.		4.	
a. ____ big		a. ____ sleepy	
b. ____ bigger		b. ____ sleepier	
c. ____ biggest		c. ____ sleepiest	

Now, draw two sets of pictures. Use words that have the **er** and **est** endings. Label your drawing like the giraffes above.

Endings and Possessives

Think about how the words in dark print are the same.

Tall is to **taller** and **tallest** as **long** is to **longer** and **longest**.

Tall-taller-tallest are comparing things by using the endings **er** and **est**.

Long-longer-longest are comparing things by using the endings **er** and **est**.

Read the examples. Look at the endings. Write the missing word on the line.

1. Wide is to wider and widest as loud is to louder

   and _____.

2. Fast is to faster and fastest as quick is to quicker

   and _____.

3. Old is to older and oldest as bright is to brighter

   and _____.

Challenge

4. High is to _____ and highest as _____ is to colder and coldest.

5. _____ is to kinder and kindest as nice is to nicer

   and _____.

6. Sick is to sicker and _____ as neat is to _____ and neatest.

7. Proud is to _____ and proudest as _____ is to calmer and calmest.

8. _____ is to icier and iciest as funny is to _____ and funniest.

<table>
<tr><td>Endings and Possessives</td><td>To show that an object belongs to one person or thing, add **'s** to the end of the word.</td></tr>
</table>

Endings and Possessives

To show that an object belongs to one person or thing, add **'s** to the end of the word.

teacher   desk = teacher's desk

To show that an object belongs to more than one person or thing, add an **'** after the last **s**.

girls   house   = girls' house

Read the story. Does it sound silly?

I slept over at the house of my friend last night. It was fun! We had pizza for dinner, then played in the room of his brothers. His brothers weren't home because they were at the house of their grandma. Next, we rode in the car of his mother to the store. When we got home we watched T.V. and played with the computer of his father. Finally, it was time for bed. We were so tired that we didn't get up until the alarm clock of his sister rang the next morning.

Rewrite the story on the lines using possessives. Add **'s** or **s'** to show what belongs to the persons in the story. The first sentence has been done for you.

I slept over at my friend's house last night.

_____

_____

_____

_____

_____

_____

_____

_____

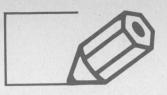

Webster and Arnold had a good time playing in their bunk-bed cave. On the lines below, write a story about a good time you had with your brother, sister, cousin, or best friend.

_____

_____

_____

_____

_____

_____

_____

_____

_____

_____

_____

_____

Write the base word for each numbered word in the correct spaces. The circled letters will tell you what learning about endings helps you do. Write the circled letters on the lines.

1. waiting
2. scrubbed
3. fitting
4. skates
5. voting
6. shopping

7. empties
8. joked
9. tripped
10. smiling
11. begged
12. asked

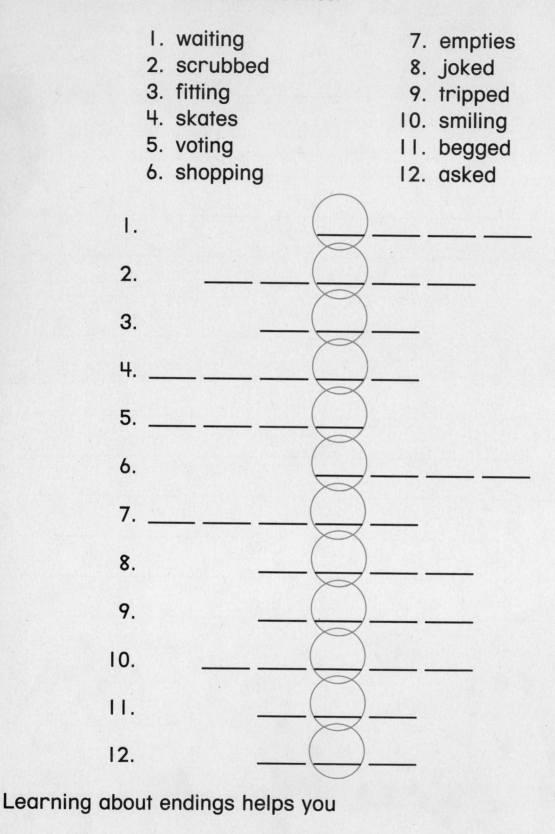

1. ___ ___ ___ ___ ___

2. ___ ___ ___ ___ ___

3. ___ ___ ___

4. ___ ___ ___ ___ ___

5. ___ ___ ___

6. ___ ___ ___ ___

7. ___ ___ ___ ___

8. ___ ___ ___

9. ___ ___ ___

10. ___ ___ ___ ___

11. ___ ___

12. ___ ___

Learning about endings helps you

___ ___ ___ ___ ___ ___ ___ ___ ___ ___ ___ ___ .
 1   2   3   4   5   6   7   8   9 10 11 12

Read each base word. Then, read the new words with endings. Fill in the circle under the word that is spelled correctly.

1. deny	denying ○	dening ○
2. wish	wishes ○	wishs ○
3. jump	jumping ○	jumpping ○
4. pass	passied ○	passed ○
5. swim	swimming ○	swiming ○
6. trace	traceed ○	traced ○
7. beg	beging ○	begging ○
8. ask	asked ○	askked ○

Endings and Possessives   **199**

Read each sentence that has been started for you. Then fill in the circle under the word that completes the sentence.

1. Move the _____ to the back of the classroom.

    desks   deskes
      ○   ○

2. Help! I see two gray _____.

    mice   mouses
      ○   ○

3. Are these redwoods the _____ trees in the forest?

    taller   tallest
      ○   ○

4. The _____ hat was blown off by the strong wind.

    boys'   boy's
      ○   ○

5. Marty _____ with his little brother.

    plaied   played
      ○   ○

6. We _____ for the bus for over an hour.

    waitted   waited
      ○   ○

7. Will you do some _____ after school?

    shoping   shopping
      ○   ○

8. Have you _____ the pencil sharpener yet?

    emptied   emptyed
      ○   ○

Frosted Glass

Gregory touched the window. The glass was cold and frosty. He drew the sun. "Gregory," said the teacher. "Please come to the front of the room and draw a circle for the class." Gregory drew a circle.

"It looks like a flat tire," said Donald laughing.

Gregory took out his crayons. He sat them neatly at the top of his desk. Adrienne gave Gregory a piece of drawing paper.

"Today," said the teacher, "we're going to draw a vase and flowers. We call this a 'still life.' Please begin."

Gregory drew his picture carefully. He turned the picture upside down. Upside down the flowers looked like flames, and the vase looked like a rocket ship. Gregory added fins. He drew spinning planets and flashing comets in the night sky. He filled the darkness with tiny stars.

The bell rang. "Time to go," said the teacher. Gregory walked down the hall. He climbed on the bus next to the window. Adrienne jumped on the bus and flopped down next to Gregory.

"I had to help the teacher put up our pictures," she sighed. "You should see them. Mine's so-so. But yours—you should see it. The teacher put it right in the middle of all the flowers. It's beautiful. The teacher said so. I love it."

Gregory smiled. He touched the window. The glass was cold and frosty. Gregory drew a circle. It was perfect.

—Denys Cazet

People see things in different ways. To Gregory, the flowers and the vase looked like a rocket ship launching into outer space.

Look at the triangle. What does it look like to you? Maybe a tepee or a big pointed hat? What if you turn the page upside down like Gregory did? Create your own picture. Share it with your classmates. Are your pictures the same or different?

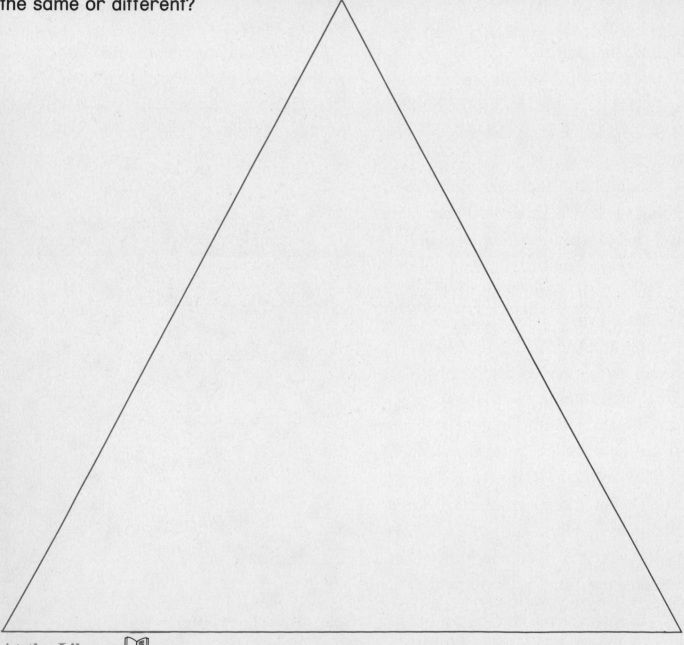

At the Library 📖

If you would like to read more about using your imagination, read these books.

<u>Anno's Alphabet: An Adventure in Imagination</u> by Mitsumasa Anno

<u>Harold and the Purple Crayon</u> by Crockett Johnson

Read the sentences from the story. Some of the words are missing. Fill in the missing words so the sentences make sense.

1. Gregory touched the window. The glass was

   cold and _____.

2. Gregory took out his crayons. He sat them _____ at the top of his desk.

3. Gregory drew his picture _____.

4. Gregory smiled. He touched the window. The glass was

   cold and _____.

Family Activity

A prefix is a syllable added to the beginning of a word. Add the prefix **un** to the beginning of these words: **happy**, **tie**, **kind**, and **cover**. How does the meaning change? A suffix is a syllable added to the end of a word. Add the suffix **y** to these words: **rain**, **luck**, **room**, **health**. Write the new words. How does the meaning change?

| Prefixes and Suffixes | A suffix is a syllable added to the end of a word. It changes the meaning of the word. |

The suffix **ful** means **full of**: **painful** means **full of pain**.
The suffix **less** means **without**: **painless** means **without pain**.
Painful and **painless** are opposites.

Read each sentence. Circle the word that has a suffix.
Then write the opposite of the circled word on the line.
The first one is done for you.

1. The ballerina was (graceful) as she danced across the stage.

   graceless

2. The artist's paintings were bright and colorful.

   _____

3. The bookshelf that Sondra and her father built is very useful.

   _____

4. In the play, I was the fearless king who ruled the land.

   _____

5. Susan and her mother fixed the helpless bird's wing.

   _____

6. The swimmer's powerful arms paddled through the water.

   _____

7. The class is hopeful that Jessica's story will win an award.

   _____

8. You should never be careless when you go horseback riding.

   _____

The suffix **y** can mean **having** or **full of**.
The suffix **ly** can mean **in a certain way**.

Read each sentence. Add the suffix **y** or **ly** to each word.
Then write the word on the line to complete the sentence.

1. _____ everyone doesn't get to be in the school play, but this year was different.   Usual

2. Some boys and girls _____ worked on the scenery.   quiet

3. It was important to practice reading our lines loudly and _____.   slow

4. Eric had the part of the _____ frog.   sleep

5. Janet was playing the role of the _____ princess.   fuss

6. We were _____ to find an old box full of costumes.   luck

7. The tickets Mrs. Newsom kept in her desk would come in _____.   hand

8. We _____ wrote out invitations to send to our friends.   neat

9. The stage was _____ lit as the audience waited.   bright

10. _____ the curtain went up!   Sudden

A prefix is a syllable added to the beginning of a word. It changes the meaning of the word. The prefix **un** means **not**, or **opposite of**. The prefix **re** means **again**, or **do over**. Look at each picture. Add the prefixes **re** and **un** to the picture word. Write the two new words on the lines.

1.   cover

_____

_____

2.   pack

_____

_____

3.   wind

_____

_____

4.   lock

_____

_____

Read each word. Add the prefix **un** or **re** to the word and write the new word on the line. Remember **un** means **not** and **re** means **again**.

1. fair _____

2. safe _____

3. tell _____

4. play _____

5. heat _____

6. true _____

7. use _____

8. happy _____

Gregory could draw when he was drawing for himself but not when he was drawing for the class. Have you ever had a similar experience? Write about it.

_____

_____

_____

_____

_____

_____

_____

_____

_____

_____

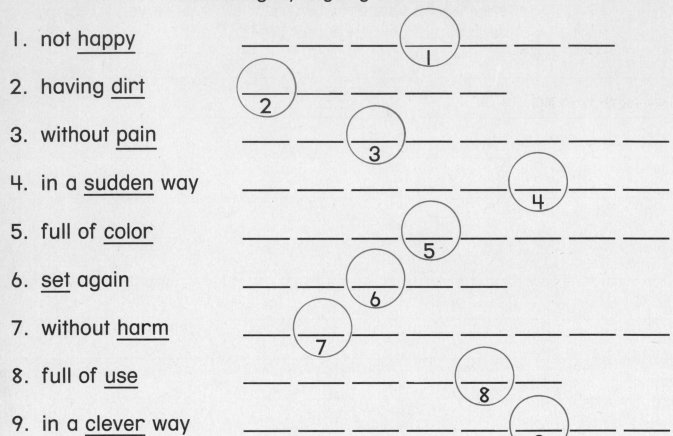

| Prefixes and Suffixes | Read each meaning. Add the prefix **un** or **re**, or the suffix **y**, **ly**, **less** or **ful** to each underlined word. Then write the new word on the lines. Use the circled letters to find out what Gregory is going to draw next. |

1. not <u>happy</u>   ___ ___ ___ ⟨1⟩ ___ ___ ___ ___

2. having <u>dirt</u>   ⟨2⟩ ___ ___ ___ ___

3. without <u>pain</u>   ___ ⟨3⟩ ___ ___ ___ ___ ___ ___

4. in a <u>sudden</u> way   ___ ___ ___ ___ ⟨4⟩ ___ ___

5. full of <u>color</u>   ___ ___ ___ ___ ⟨5⟩ ___ ___ ___

6. <u>set</u> again   ___ ___ ⟨6⟩ ___ ___ ___

7. without <u>harm</u>   ___ ⟨7⟩ ___ ___ ___ ___ ___

8. full of <u>use</u>   ___ ___ ___ ___ ⟨8⟩ ___

9. in a <u>clever</u> way   ___ ___ ___ ___ ___ ⟨9⟩ ___ ___

___ ___ ___ ___ ___ ___ ___ ___ ___
1   2   3   4   5   6   7   8   9

Read the word at the beginning of each row. Then fill in the circle under the word that has the same suffix or prefix.

1. helpful	fill ○	replay ○	careful ○	fussy ○
2. careless	fearless ○	carnival ○	lessen ○	minus ○
3. frosty	toasted ○	windy ○	snowstorm ○	frog ○
4. quickly	sadly ○	painless ○	speedy ○	quiet ○
5. untie	unite ○	unlock ○	tire ○	funny ○
6. redo	read ○	doing ○	write ○	repay ○
7. cheerful	cheery ○	sadly ○	powerful ○	happy ○

Prefixes and Suffixes

Read each sentence that has been started for you. Then fill in the circle under the word that completes the sentence.

1. Let me _____ your glass with milk.

refill   tasteless   cups   frosty
  ○   ○   ○   ○

2. The gym is _____ enough for the dance.

car   fitness   softly   roomy
 ○   ○   ○   ○

3. That creepy insect is really _____.

harmless   quickly   rainy   skillful
  ○   ○   ○   ○

4. Don't _____ your seatbelt until the car stops.

tie   careful   undress   unbuckle
 ○   ○   ○   ○

5. The apples were crisp and _____.

baker   flavorful   unable   cheerful
 ○   ○   ○   ○

6. Heather _____ walked across the stage to get her award.

proudly   danced   colorful   careless
  ○   ○   ○   ○

7. The airplane landed twice to _____.

speedy   refuel   slowly   healthy
  ○   ○   ○   ○

8. A toothache can be _____.

unpleasant   hurt   sadly   windy
   ○   ○   ○   ○

Alexander and the Terrible, Horrible, No Good, Very Bad Day

I went to sleep with gum in my mouth and now there's gum in my hair and when I got out of bed this morning I tripped on the skateboard and by mistake I dropped my sweater in the sink while the water was running and I could tell it was going to be a terrible, horrible, no good, very bad day.

At breakfast Anthony found a Corvette Sting Ray car kit in his breakfast cereal box and Nick found a Junior Undercover Agent code ring in his breakfast cereal box but in my breakfast cereal box all I found was breakfast cereal.

I think I'll move to Australia.

At school Mrs. Dickens liked Paul's picture of the sailboat better than my picture of the invisible castle. I could tell it was going to be a terrible, horrible, no good, very bad day.

That's what is was, because after school my mom took us all to the dentist and Dr. Fields found a cavity just in me. Come back next week and I'll fix it, said Dr. Fields. Next week, I said, I'm going to Australia.

There were lima beans for dinner and I hate limas.

There was kissing on TV and I hate kissing.

It has been a terrible, horrible, no good, very bad day.

My mom says some days are like that. Even in Australia.

—Judith Viorst

Everyone has "terrible, horrible, no good, very bad days." List words that describe one of yours.

_____

_____

_____

_____

_____

_____

_____

_____

_____

_____

_____

_____

At the Library 📖

Read these books about good days and bad days.
Mr. Gumpy's Outing by John Burningham

Some of the Days of Everett Anderson by Lucille Clifton

Read the sentences. Some of the words are missing. Fill in the missing words so the sentences make sense.

1. I tripped on the skateboard and by mistake I dropped my sweater in the sink while the water was running and I could tell it was going to be a

_____, _____, ___ _____, _____ _____ day.

2. At school Mrs. Dickens liked Paul's picture of the sailboat better than my picture of the invisible castle. I could tell it was going to be a

_____, _____, ___ _____, _____ _____ day.

3. There were lima beans for dinner and I hate limas. There was kissing on TV and I hate kissing. It has been a

_____, _____, ___ _____, _____ _____ day.

Family Activity

Make a list of some nice things you can do for someone who's having a terrible day. Then write some other words that have the same meaning as the word *nice*.

Synonyms are words that have almost the same meaning. Read each sentence. Write the synonym for the word in parentheses on the line.

1. The teacher asked me to _____ the door.
   (close)

   open   shut   lock   clap

2. The horse had to _____ over the fence.
   (jump)

   trot   run   gallop   leap

3. The water in our swimming pool was very _____.
   (cool)

   clean   warm   cold   blue

4. Alice put on her _____ and went outside.
   (coat)

   hat   sweater   boots   jacket

5. I saw a _____ puppy in the window of the pet shop.
   (little)

   small   big   black   large

6. On the playground, the boys and girls _____.
   (shouted)

   played   talked   yelled   jumped

7. My dad reads the newspaper every _____.
   (evening)

   day   night   morning   week

8. Be careful when you go across the _____!
   (street)

   store   walk   stop   road

Play tic-tac-toe. Draw a straight line through three words in each game that are synonyms. You can go across, down, or corner to corner.

tall	thin	stare
book	see	need
look	like	find

fast	race	car
last	quick	quilt
run	slow	speedy

Now make your own tic-tac-toe game. Fill in the squares with words. Be sure to put three words that are synonyms in a straight line. Give your game to a friend to play.

| Synonyms, Antonyms, and Homonyms | **Antonyms** are words that mean the opposite of each other. *Hard* and *soft* are antonyms, so are over and under. Write an antonym for each word in parentheses so the letter Richy wrote to his friend makes sense. The first one has been done for you. |

Dear Tommy,

_____Hi_____! How are you? I was _____ that I had
(Bye)   (glad)

to move away. I miss playing with you _____ school.
(before)

I go to a _____ school now. My teacher is very
(old)

_____. Her name is Mrs. Roberts. She _____
(mean)   (always)

gives us homework. I _____ next to my friend Jimmy.
(stand)

My class is learning all about _____ space. It's fun!
(inner)

My new house has a _____ backyard. Now my
(small)

mom lets us play baseball and soccer. And I have my

very own room.

Please write soon.

Your Friend,

Richy

P.S. You're still my _____ friend.
(worst)

Find the pair of antonyms used in each riddle. Write them
on the lines next to the riddle. Then answer the riddle.

1. You can walk right through me.
   Use me to go in and out.
   _____

   I am a _____.
   _____

2. I am something you always hang up.
   With me you can talk to friends near or far.
   _____

   I am a _____.
   _____

3. When you turn me on, it's nice and bright.
   When you turn me off, there is no light.
   _____

   I am a _____.
   _____

4. I go up hills and down hills.
   But I never move.
   _____

   I am a _____.
   _____

5. Everyone has a first and last.
   I am what you call yourself.
   _____

   I am your _____.
   _____

6. You only see me when the sun is shining.
   I may be tall or short.
   _____

   I am your _____.
   _____

Make up your own riddle. Give it to a friend to solve.

_____

_____

Homonyms are words that sound the same but have different meanings and different spellings. *Sale* and *sail* are homonyms. So are *meat* and *meet*. Read each sentence. Write the correct homonym on the line.

1. The wind _____ my _____ hat off.

   blue
   blew

2. I _____ my bike down the dirt _____.

   rode
   road

3. Do you _____ if the answer is

   yes or _____?

   no
   know

4. Dad got _____ books _____ you at the library.

   four
   for

5. Jan will _____ the door and try on her

   new _____.

   clothes
   close

6. _____ you like to get more _____ for the campfire?

   would
   wood

7. Neil can only _____ with his

   _____ hand.

   right
   write

8. Come over _____ so I can _____ what you're saying.

   hear
   here

Challenge

Write the homonyms for these words: **peak**, **sea**, **son**, **weak**, **flour**, **knows**, **hare**, and **tale**.

Read the story. Circle the words that don't make sense. Write a homonym for each word you have circled on the lines below the story.

Sharon and her mother were going shopping. There had been a big sail at the store all weak.

Sharon needed a new pear of shoes. She tried on won shoe at a time. But none of the shoes fit her tiny feat. Finally, they found a pair she could where. She was so excited that she could hardly weight for her friends to sea them.

1. _____   2. _____   3. _____

4. _____   5. _____   6. _____

7. _____   8. _____

Write some sentences of your own using homonyms. The words in the box will help you get started.

tail	tale	cent	sent
hair	hare	dear	deer

1. _____

2. _____

3. _____

4. _____

Synonyms, Antonyms, and Homonyms   219

Read each sentence. Then write an antonym, synonym, or homonym for the word in parentheses.

antonym   1. When I woke _____ this morning the
                        (down)

sun was shining.

homonym   2. I ate _____ pancakes, dripping in
                   (to)

maple syrup, for breakfast.

antonym   3. On my way to school I _____ a quarter.
                                    (lost)

antonym   4. Mrs. Jones didn't even notice that I

_____ my homework.
(remembered)

homonym   5. A _____ fireman came to visit our class.
                 (reel)

synonym   6. In gym class, I ran the _____ in the
                                     (fastest)

50 yard dash.

antonym   7. After school, my friend let me _____ with
                                             (work)

his new dinosaur.

synonym   8. I had a _____ day!
                     (great)

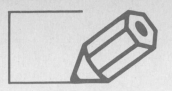

Alexander really didn't move to Australia. He knew the next day might be just the opposite of the terrible, horrible, no good, very bad day. Write about Alexander's terrific, wonderful, just great, very good day.

When I woke up this morning _____

_____

_____

_____

At breakfast _____

_____

_____

At school _____

_____

_____

After school _____

_____

_____

At dinner _____

_____

_____

After dinner _____

_____

_____

Read each clue. Then write the answer in the correct spaces in the puzzle.

ACROSS

1. Antonym of tall
3. Homonym of maid
4. Homonym of blew
5. Synonym of jacket

DOWN

1. Synonym of little
2. Antonym of under
3. Homonym of meet
4. Antonym of front

Finish each sentence.

An antonym is _____

A synonym is _____

A homonym is _____

_____

Read the first word in each row. Then fill in the circle
under the word that is an antonym.

1. quiet	talk ○	queen ○	loud ○	stop ○
2. right	write ○	left ○	night ○	win ○
3. wet	dry ○	damp ○	water ○	pet ○
4. fast	quick ○	last ○	race ○	slow ○

Read the first word in each row. Then fill in the circle
under the word that is a synonym.

5. shut	ship ○	open ○	door ○	close ○
6. jump	play ○	jacket ○	hop ○	just ○
7. boat	coat ○	ship ○	road ○	swim ○
8. sleep	rest ○	slip ○	keep ○	glad ○

Read each sentence that has been started for you. Then fill in the circle under the word that completes the sentence.

1. I got a new _____ of mittens.

    pair   pear
     ○   ○

2. The dog barked and wagged its _____.

    tale   tail
     ○   ○

3. There are seven days in a _____.

    week   weak
     ○   ○

4. Tim's brother just turned _____ years old.

    four   for
     ○   ○

5. Jane had a pretty ribbon in her _____.

    hare   hair
     ○   ○

6. I can _____ better with my glasses.

    sea   see
     ○   ○

7. Is there _____ on your sandwich?

    meet   meat
     ○   ○